"Tom Lutz guides those who guide others in faithful living by writing, 'The law was never about earning God's favor . . . it is a natural response to the grace we have already received in Christ. . . . The result of following the law is spiritual growth, greater intimacy with God, and alignment with His purposes for our lives and the world.' Such clear gospel motivation is rare in books about discipleship, making this book a blessing for those who will use it to guide others in grateful, faithful, and blessed responses to the grace that is in Christ Jesus."

—Bryan Chapell

President, Unlimited Grace Media

Author of *Christ-centered Preaching*

"In *Equipping Christians for Kingdom Obedience* Tom Lutz firmly dispels the myth of the law being a harsh taskmaster. Rather he proves the case that the law is not just a guide, but the guide for a Christian who truly wants to become like Christ, living a godly life. The reflection questions are painfully profound. They dig deep and should be thoughtfully answered by the reader of this essential book for spiritual growth."

—Randy Schlichting DMin

President Metro Atlanta Seminary

"Building on the Reformation emphasis on the law as a guide towards human flourishing, Tom Lutz brings the doctrine to life through a profound and practical biblical overview of the law's relevance and blessing for followers of Christ today. Rooted in the gospel, Dr. Lutz traces the thread of the law's blessings to and through God's people through the tapestry of redemptive history, while helping all of us see God's gracious heart in the call to obedience in the realities of everyday life. This book is a great blessing to all who seek to find the delight of following Christ."

—Ryan Brown
Executive Director of Life on Life Ministries

"In *Equipping Christians for Kingdom Obedience: A Guide for All Who Make Disciples,* Tom Lutz moves the reader from purpose to practice, centering the Decalogue as the timeless moral compass for believers transformed by grace. This work illuminates how God's Law—rooted in the Creation Mandate and fulfilled in Christ—guides the believer through the Being-Knowing-Doing framework, convicting, bridling, and directing us toward holiness without the burden of legalism.

As Director of Doctoral Studies at Metro Atlanta Seminary and a discipleship coach for pastors and churches, I am encouraged by the integration of theology with practical ministry. Tom offers a biblical-theological anchor for training leaders to obey God's commands as a response to His covenant grace, not a means to earn it. It challenges the Pharisaic distortions of the Law while affirming its enduring role in spiritual maturity, making it an invaluable resource for seminary instruction and pastoral coaching.

I wholeheartedly endorse *Equipping Christians for Kingdom Obedience.* In an age of moral ambiguity, this guide restores the Law's beauty as a pathway to liberty and flourishing, empowering believers to live as image-bearers who honor God and bless others."

—Dr. Robert Jolly

Director of Doctoral Studies at Metro Atlanta Seminary

"The Ten Commandments are a treasured piece of my devotional life that I pray through weekly, asking God to not only help me avoid breaking them, but to positively apply them in every area of my life. These prayers might look something like, 'Help me to make you #1 in my life God, and to avoid all forms of idolatry. Give me grace to love my mom and dad, to rest, and to lovingly pursue my wife; help me to be generous, and to forgive rather than hold angry grudges so that I might bear true witness to you.' I know of no better way of keeping a check on myself than by regularly praying through the Ten Commandments. That said, I am excited about Tom's book coming out! The Ten Commandments are still vitally important, the only part of Scripture ever written directly by the Hand of God, and yet they are so thoroughly misunderstood, disregarded, or even seen as backwards by many Christians! Tom's book will help believers to know the why and the how for these sacred words that are completely relevant today, and how people can build their lives on them. It is my prayer that Tom's words go 'round the world' to help inform the lives and prayers of every reader who picks up this book on the Ten Commandments!"

—Adam Whitescarver

Executive Director of Pray Chattanooga

Pastor at Red Bank Cumberland Presbyterian Church

Equipping Christians *for* KINGDOM OBEDIENCE

A GUIDE FOR ALL WHO MAKE DISCIPLES

TOM LUTZ

CLAY BRIDGES PRESS

Equipping Christians for Kingdom Obedience

A Guide for All Who Make Disciples

Published by Clay Bridges Press in Houston, TX
www.ClayBridgesPress.com

ISBN: 978-1-68488-172-7
eISBN: 978-1-68488-173-4

Special Sales: Most Clay Bridges titles are available in special quantity discounts. Custom imprinting or excerpting can also be done to fit special needs. Contact Clay Bridges at Info@ClayBridgesPress.com.

To the students of Metro Atlanta Seminary
who always encourage me by practicing what I preach.

CONTENTS

Preface: Building on Kingdom Discipleship xi

Chapter 1: The Purpose and Significance of the Law..........1

Chapter 2: The Law in the Old Testament:
The Foundation..11

Chapter 3: The "Then" and the "Now":
The Uniqueness of God's Speech and
the Application of the Law 19

Chapter 4: The "Then" and the "Now":
The Uniqueness of God's Speech and the
Application of the Law (Commands 1–4) 29

Chapter 5: The "Then" and the "Now":
The Uniqueness of God's Speech and the
Application of the Law (Commands 5–10) 35

Chapter 6: Wisdom Literature: The Practical
Application of the Law in Daily Life 41

Chapter 7: The Law in the Psalms: An Integral
Foundation for Worship.................................51

Chapter 8: Proverbs – The Settled Application of God's Law in Daily Life 59

Chapter 9: The Proverbs 31 Woman – A Life of Covenant Faithfulness 69

Chapter 10: The Book of Lamentations: God's Faithfulness Amidst Judgment 79

Chapter 11: The Revival Under Ezra and Nehemiah: Returning to the Decalogue 89

Chapter 12: The Sermon on the Mount: Jesus Restores the True Meaning of the Law 97

Chapter 13: Romans and the Being, Knowing, Doing Framework 109

Chapter 14: The Law in the Book of James: Living Out the Law of Liberty 119

Chapter 15: The Law and the New Covenant: The Believer's Responsibility to the Law 129

Chapter 16: Practical Application for Today: Understanding the Role of the Law in the Believer's Life 137

Epilogue: A Legacy of Obedience: "Be Careful to Obey" 145

Acknowledgments 151

About the Author 153

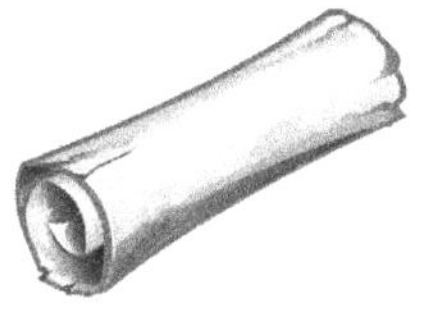

Preface:

BUILDING ON KINGDOM DISCIPLESHIP

In *Equipping Christians for Kingdom Purpose in Their Work: A Guide for All Who Make Disciples*, I focused on helping believers understand their identity as image-bearers of God and how that shapes their calling and purpose in the workplace. I asked the following three critical questions that framed the discussion:

- Who am I? The answer is simple: I am an image-bearer of God.
- What is my Kingdom Purpose? My purpose encompasses glorifying God, blessing others, and contributing to the flourishing of God's creation through every form of work—whether paid or unpaid.
- How will I fulfill my purpose? I fulfill my purpose by actively living out my Kingdom Purpose in the

> world where I engage with others and demonstrate God's love through my vocations.

The focus of that book was to equip those whose vocation or avocation is to disciple others, particularly within the context of work. I aimed to empower disciplers to see their own work and ministry as part of God's larger Kingdom narrative and to guide others in discovering how to integrate their faith into their daily work.

This current book, *Equipping Christians for Kingdom Obedience: A Guide for All Who Make Disciples*, is a natural continuation of that work. It builds on the foundation laid in *Equipping Christians for Kingdom Purpose in Their Work* by shifting the focus to a deeper understanding of the law—particularly the law as expressed in the Decalogue—and its role in shaping the life of every believer. While the first book helped individuals connect their work with God's eternal Kingdom purpose, this book explores how to live faithfully within the framework of God's moral law, as revealed in both the Old and New Testaments.

Much like the earlier work, this book calls us to view our actions and decisions—whether in the workplace, at home, or in the community—as an expression of our relationship with God. However, we now broaden our view to include a more comprehensive understanding of how God's law acts as a guide, convicting us and enabling us to live lives that reflect His character and bring His Kingdom to earth.

For those familiar with *Equipping Christians for Kingdom Purpose in Their Work*, this book will build on the strategies and methods discussed in that work, showing how the law—especially the Decalogue—serves as a crucial tool for discipleship. In the context of the Kingdom, the law is not a burden but a guide that leads to freedom, peace, and flourishing. By carefully observing God's commands, believers become equipped to live in accordance with their redeemed identity and fulfill their divine calling.

One key difference between this book and the first is that while *Equipping Christians for Kingdom Purpose in Their Work* focused primarily on the first two questions—Who am I? and What is my Kingdom Purpose?—this book expands especially on the third question: How will I fulfill my purpose? While the first book provided practical strategies for integrating faith and work, this book deepens the understanding of how God's law plays a central role in fulfilling that purpose. It not only provides theological depth but also equips believers to implement this understanding through the same strategies and methods introduced in the earlier work.

In this book, I continue to ask: Who are we as God's redeemed image-bearers? How can we live out our purpose through obedience to God's law and the ongoing work of His Kingdom?

The framework for this work remains the same: It is not just about internalizing a set of rules; it is about living out the very life of Christ in a fallen world. As we explore the relationship among the law, the gospel, and the believer's daily life, I invite you to walk through Scripture to see how the law serves as a road map for every disciple committed to living out their Kingdom Purpose in this world.

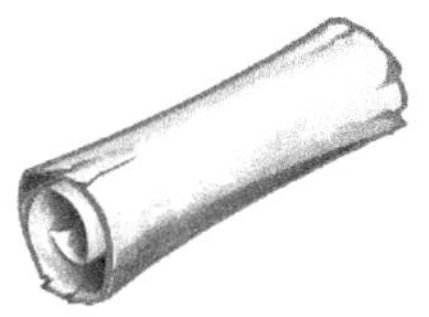

Chapter 1:
THE PURPOSE AND SIGNIFICANCE OF THE LAW

The law of God is not merely a set of rules or ancient codes designed to govern the people of Israel. It is much deeper. It is an expression of God's holiness and a foundation for the covenantal relationship between God and His people. From the very beginning, the law was meant to guide, shape, and transform humanity's relationship with its Creator. To truly understand the significance of the law, we must begin at the very foundation of humanity itself, with the Creation Mandate.

The Creation Mandate: Humanity's Original Purpose

In the opening chapters of Genesis, God creates humanity in His image and commissions them with a mandate to be stewards of His creation. This is what I call the Creation Mandate—the original purpose God gave to humanity. In Genesis

1:26, God says, "Let us make mankind in our image, in our likeness, so that they may rule over the fish in the sea and the birds in the sky, over the livestock and all the wild animals."

From the beginning, humanity was created to reflect God's character in the world. As image-bearers, we are meant to reflect God's holiness, justice, mercy, and truth. Our role is not only to worship and enjoy God but to cultivate and steward the earth. We are co-laborers with God, tasked with bringing order, beauty, and flourishing to the creation that He made. This is the cultural mandate—to work, create, and care for the earth in ways that reflect God's glory and goodness.

This mandate speaks to the purpose of human existence. We are to reflect God's image, care for His creation, and live in harmony with one another and the world He created. The law given later in Scripture provides a means to guide us in living out this mandate, offering moral and ethical principles that direct how we engage with the world and one another.

The Law as a Guiding Principle

After the fall, humanity's understanding of this mandate was distorted, and the world became marred by sin, brokenness, and rebellion. Yet God did not abandon His original design. The law given to Israel, beginning with the Ten Commandments in Exodus 19–20, is a restoration of that mandate. The law shows how to live out the cultural mandate within the brokenness of the world.

The Decalogue, or Ten Words, given by God directly to the people of Israel is foundational because it encapsulates the moral order of the world—God's original design for humanity. The law calls humanity back to the original intention for life in the world, which is to live in a way that reflects God's holiness and His purpose for creation. That is why the law is not just a list of commands but a way to live as image-bearers in a fallen world, drawing us back into the original purpose for which we were created.

The Mandate of Obedience: Rooted in the Old Testament, Fulfilled in Christ

From the earliest days of Israel's journey, the concept of "careful obedience" to God's commands has been foundational to the identity of His redeemed people. In Deuteronomy, Moses emphasizes to the Israelites that their obedience to God's laws would not only ensure their flourishing in the Promised Land but would also set them apart as a wise and understanding nation, reflecting God's holiness to the surrounding peoples (Deut. 4:5–6). This call to diligent obedience was passed from one generation to the next—Moses to Joshua (Josh. 1:7), David to Solomon (1 Kings 2:3), and Solomon to the people (1 Chron. 28:8). Even in times of exile, the prophets continued to urge God's people to remain faithful to His commands, assuring them that their obedience was vital to their restoration (Jer. 29:4 7, Ezek. 36:26 27).

The careful observance of God's laws was not merely a

personal matter but a cultural responsibility, ensuring that the covenant community would reflect His character, fulfill the cultural mandate, and actively contribute to the flourishing of the world around them. Ultimately, Jesus culminates this trend in the Great Commission, commanding His disciples to "go and make disciples of all nations . . . teaching them to obey everything I have commanded you" (Matt. 28:19–20). In this way, the call to obedient living extends beyond Israel, encompassing all nations as part of God's redemptive plan for the world.

The Three Frameworks: A Guide to Understanding the Law

Before delving into the specifics of how the law functions, it is important to introduce three frameworks that will guide our understanding throughout this book. These frameworks help explain how the law shapes the believer's life and how it is to be lived out in the context of faith.

Being, Knowing, Doing: This framework outlines the progression of the Christian life.

Being refers to our identity in Christ. The law is a guide for those who have been transformed by Christ and empowered by the Holy Spirit to live as image-bearers in the world. Only when our Being has been changed—when we have been justified and adopted as children of God—can we properly understand and follow the law as a guide for living. The law is not a means to earn favor but a reflection of the new identity we have in Christ.

Knowing refers to our understanding of God's will, revealed in the law. The law teaches us what is pleasing to God and helps us understand the moral and spiritual principles that govern His Kingdom.

Doing refers to how we live out that knowledge in obedience to God's commands. The law guides us in how we are to live and act in the world as faithful stewards of God's creation.

Effort vs. Earning: The law is often misunderstood as a way to earn God's favor—a checklist of rules to follow to gain acceptance. However, the law was never about earning God's favor; it is about effort in response to God's grace. We are empowered by the Holy Spirit to obey the law, but that obedience is not a means of earning God's love. Rather, it is a natural response to the grace we have already received in Christ. The effort to live according to God's law reflects our desire to grow in holiness and to reflect God's character.

Result vs. Reward: The law is not a transactional system in which we obey in order to gain a reward. Rather, it is a way of life that produces spiritual results. Obedience to the law leads to peace, joy, and godliness, not as rewards for our actions but as the natural result of living according to God's will. The result of following the law is spiritual growth, greater intimacy with God, and alignment with His purposes for our lives and the world.

The Role of the Law in the New Covenant

In the New Covenant, the law is not abolished but fulfilled in Christ. Jesus came to restore humanity's broken relationship with God, and His life, death, and resurrection revealed the full meaning of God's law. Jesus deepened the understanding of the law, not by nullifying it but by teaching its spiritual depth—that the heart of the law is not just external obedience but a transformation of the heart and mind to reflect God's love and righteousness.

In the Sermon on the Mount, Jesus does not reinterpret the law; He shows that the law was always about heart transformation. Jesus reveals that obedience to God's commands is not about rule-following but about living in alignment with God's will in a way that honors His image in the world. The Sermon on the Mount demonstrates that the law is not merely about avoiding wrong actions but about loving God and loving our neighbors as the fulfillment of God's law.

The Law as a Reflection of God's Holiness

Ultimately, the law is a reflection of God's holiness. It shows us what it means to live as image-bearers in the world. The law guides us back to the holiness that God desires for His people, and as believers in Christ, we are empowered by the Holy Spirit to live out that holiness. The law is not a burden but a blessing—a way for God's people to reflect His character in the world and to participate in His mission of restoration and reconciliation.

Through Christ, believers are now able to live out the law in the power of the Spirit, not to gain favor with God but because they have already been made righteous by faith. This transformation in the believer's life is the fulfillment of the law in the New Covenant.

The Law and the Creation Mandate Today

The Creation Mandate calls humanity to work, cultivate, and steward the earth, reflecting God's image in all that we do. The law provides guidance on how this mandate is to be lived out, not just in ancient Israel but in the lives of God's people today. It is through the moral guidance of the law that we continue to fulfill our role as image-bearers in a broken world.

The law teaches us how to live in relationship with God and one another, ensuring justice, mercy, and love are reflected in all aspects of life. Today, as believers in Christ, we are called to live according to the moral principles of the law in our own lives, not through legalistic rule-following but through a transformed heart that reflects God's holiness and His will for the world.

Conclusion: Living Out the Law as Image-Bearers

The law given to Israel is not an outdated relic of an ancient time; it is the eternal moral framework that reflects the nature of God and guides His people in reflecting His image in the world. It is through the law that humanity is called to live as image-bearers, fulfilling the cultural mandate to reflect God's character and care for His creation.

In the New Covenant, this law is fulfilled in Christ, and believers are empowered by the Holy Spirit to live according to God's will. The law continues to play a crucial role in guiding believers toward living lives that reflect God's holiness, justice, mercy, and love. By living out the law in the power of Christ, we are participating in God's redemptive mission to restore the world and bring it back into alignment with His perfect will.

Study Guide for Chapter 1

The Purpose and Significance of the Law

Summary:
This chapter introduces the Law as rooted in the Creation Mandate, reflecting God's holiness and guiding believers into their vocation as image-bearers.

Discussion Questions:

1. How does the Creation Mandate frame the purpose of the Law?

2. What does the Being–Knowing–Doing framework reveal about Christian obedience?

3. Why is the Law an expression of God's grace rather than a burden?

Application

Identify one area of life where obedience aligns you more closely with God's created design.

Scripture Reflection: Genesis 1:26–28

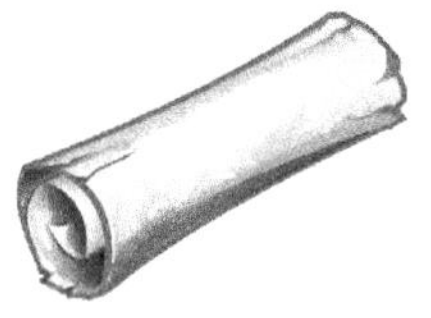

Chapter 2:
THE LAW IN THE OLD TESTAMENT: THE FOUNDATION

The law in the Old Testament is not merely a list of rules but the foundation of Israel's covenantal relationship with God. Given at Mount Sinai after the exodus from Egypt, the law defines what it means to be God's people and outlines how they are to live in response to His holiness. At its heart, the law calls Israel to reflect God's nature in their daily lives, and it serves as a guide for their spiritual, social, and moral behavior.

The Giving of the Law: Exodus 19–24

The moment God gave the law to Israel at Mount Sinai was a pivotal event in the history of the covenant. In Exodus 19, the Israelites camp at Mount Sinai, and God speaks to them, declaring that they are to be His treasured possession among all the nations. They are called to be a kingdom of priests and a holy nation (Exod. 19:5–6). In this declaration, God sets the stage for the giving of the Decalogue—the Ten Words—that will form the moral foundation of Israel's covenant with Him.

What is crucial to understand here is that God did not say, "If you keep the law perfectly, I will bring you out of slavery." Rather, God begins with a statement of grace: "I am the Lord your God, who brought you out of Egypt, out of the land of slavery" (Exod. 20:2). The law is not a condition for redemption; it is a response to the grace of God's deliverance. He freed Israel from slavery and then gave them the law as a means to live in relationship with Him and to reflect His holiness to the world.

In this way, the law is given in the context of grace from the outset. God's deliverance is not based on Israel's obedience to the law but on His unmerited favor. The imagery of God's care for Israel is portrayed in Exodus 19:4 where He compares Himself to an eagle who has carried His people on eagle's wings and brought them to Himself. Just as a mother eagle teaches her young to fly, God nurtures and guides His people into His ways, with the law as a gracious gift to shape them into a holy nation.

The Three Prerequisites to Wisdom: God's Law in the Life of His People

In Exodus 20, God begins with the Israelites' redemption before giving them the law, emphasizing that obedience follows salvation, not the other way around. God's command to "observe them carefully" (Deut. 4:5–6) introduces the foundational principles of obedience that are central to the Israelites' life in the land they are about to possess. As part of their new identity as God's redeemed people, they are called to live out the three prerequisites to wisdom: (1) an understanding of God's holiness as demonstrated by the awe-inspiring events surrounding His presence on Mount Sinai (Exod. 19); (2) the recognition of unalterable absolutes as seen in the Ten Words (the Decalogue), which stand as the foundational, unchangeable moral law; and (3) the application of God's law where wisdom is shown in the day-to-day life of the people as they live out the law's principles.

The law given in Exodus 20 includes both apodictic laws—absolute moral commands such as "you shall not murder"—and casuistic laws, specific applications of these principles to their cultural context such as the requirement for a fence around a roof to ensure the safety of others. These laws are not merely arbitrary rules; they are practical applications of God's absolute will, designed to shape a society where God's holiness is reflected in every aspect of life. Just as the Israelites were called to be a light to the nations, so too are Christians called to embody these principles in the world, showing the wisdom of God through their obedience.

The Ten Commandments: God's Moral Order

The Ten Commandments are more than a set of laws; they are a reflection of God's moral order for humanity. The commandments deal with a variety of aspects of life, but they all stem from God's nature and His desire for His people to live in faithful relationship with Him and one another. The Decalogue is not only the foundation of Israel's covenant with God but also the moral law that reflects His holiness and justice.

The Ten Words that form the moral core of the law were not merely given as rules to follow; they were given as part of a covenantal relationship that defined Israel's identity as God's people. The Decalogue is the only time in Scripture that God speaks directly to the entire people of Israel in this manner. It stands as a universal moral standard given by God Himself that still applies to humanity today.

One example of how the Decalogue shapes life can be seen in the sixth commandment: "You shall not murder" (Exod. 20:13). While this commandment certainly prohibits the taking of a life, it is broader than that. It implies that human life is sacred, and therefore, we must care for the well-being of others in every way.

An illustration of this can be found in the application of the sixth commandment in Deuteronomy 22:8 where the law requires the building of a fence around the roof of a house. In Israel, people often entertained guests on their roofs, so a fence was required to prevent anyone from falling off and potentially being injured or killed. This fence was not just a reaction to murder but an active measure to protect life. It demonstrates that the command not to murder extends beyond physical killing to preventing harm and ensuring the flourishing of others.

This principle can be applied today in the form of laws requiring safety measures such as a fence around a pool or the need for proper guardrails on a high balcony—things that actively preserve life and prevent accidents. The Decalogue calls God's people not just to avoid killing but to care for one another's safety and promote the well-being of their fellow citizens.

Deuteronomy 4:5-6: Applying the Law in Israel's Context

In Deuteronomy 4:5–6, Moses addresses the Israelites as they prepare to enter the Promised Land. He emphasizes that the law is not just a list of commandments but a guide for life that must be applied in the specific cultural and societal context of Israel. Moses tells the people that they are to follow the pattern of applying the Decalogue through words such as *mishpatim* (judgments) and *miswah* (commands), demonstrating how these principles should be lived out in their day-to-day lives.

But the Decalogue is not just a historical document; it paints a picture of the kind of world that God desires—a world where justice and flourishing are the norms for all people. Imagine a world where everyone is committed to right and just transcendent principles, where the first four commandments guide people in honoring God and living in alignment with His will. Picture a world where every human relationship is grounded in righteousness, where everyone obeys laws that are just and good (the fifth commandment).

In such a world, no one endangers others, but rather everyone looks out for the well-being of their fellow citizens (sixth commandment). Commitments are always kept, and trust is never broken (seventh commandment). There's no hoarding of possessions for selfish gain, but rather resources are shared and used in a way that causes the community to flourish (eighth commandment). There are no lies or deceit as everyone speaks the truth to one another (ninth commandment). Finally, no one seeks to be selfish or defend their own honor at the expense of others (tenth commandment).

Who would not want to live in a world like that? The law given to Israel is not an arbitrary set of rules; it is a vision for a flourishing society where God's justice, mercy, and holiness shape every interaction and decision. It is a vision that reflects God's Kingdom where peace, justice, and mutual care are the hallmarks of life.

Conclusion: The Ever-Relevant Law

The law given to Israel at Sinai, beginning with the Ten Commandments, remains relevant today as a guide for living in alignment with God's will. As the church seeks to live as God's people, the law offers timeless principles for justice, mercy, and holiness. In the New Covenant, these principles are fulfilled in Christ, but the moral order of the law continues to serve as a guide for believers who seek to live out their identity as image-bearers in a broken world.

Study Guide for Chapter 2

The Law in the Old Testament

Summary:

God gave the Law after redeeming Israel, establishing unalterable absolutes (Ten Words) and culturally specific applications (mishpatim, miswah).

Discussion Questions:

1. Why is it important that the Law was given after redemption?

2. How do case laws reveal the breadth of each commandment?

3. Which commandment's broader application most challenges modern assumptions?

Application:
Consider one commandment and list two broader implications for today.

Scripture Reflection: Deuteronomy 4:5–6

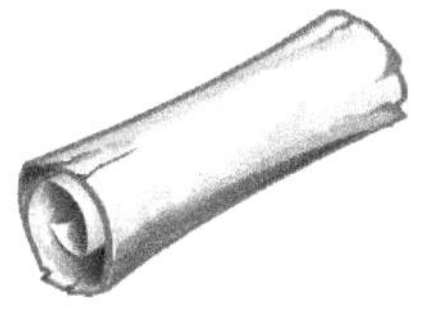

Chapter 3:

THE "THEN" AND THE "NOW": THE UNIQUENESS OF GOD'S SPEECH AND THE APPLICATION OF THE LAW

The distinction between God's direct speech in the Ten Words and the subsequent applications of those words by Moses are essential for understanding how the law operates in both ancient Israel and modern life. The Ten Words serve as a foundational moral framework, but Moses's interpretations of those words help bring them into Israel's specific historical and cultural context. This distinction highlights that while the moral principles of the Ten Words are timeless, their applications can vary as society changes.

God Speaks Directly: The Ten Words

The Ten Commandments, also known as the Ten Words, represent the only instance in the Hebrew Scriptures where God speaks directly to the entire nation of Israel. This moment is crucial in understanding the foundational nature of the law. In Exodus 20:1–17, God gives these words to Israel on Mount Sinai, a unique revelation that sets the Ten Words apart from all other laws given in Scripture. Deuteronomy 5:22 further affirms that God "added nothing" to these words, indicating their completeness and the finality of the moral principles they contain. These Ten Words serve as the bedrock for Israel's identity and the moral compass of the nation, encompassing justice, holiness, and faithfulness to God.

These principles remain central not only to Israel's covenant with God but also to our understanding of divine morality today. God's direct speech, as recorded in these commandments, provides the framework upon which all other applications of the law stand.

Moses's Role: Applying the Law in the Present

While God's Ten Words provide the moral law, Moses is tasked with applying these laws to the real-life situations the Israelites will face as they enter the Promised Land. Moses's role in applying God's commands is significant. He takes God's universal principles and interprets them for specific cultural issues. These applications are found in the Book of the Covenant (Exodus 21–23) and in Moses's speeches in Deuteronomy. The Ten

Words are not just isolated commands but moral principles that must be lived out in a society's legal and social systems.

For example, the sixth commandment ("you shall not murder") is applied in Exodus 21:18–19 with the requirement that someone who causes another person to be injured must compensate them based on the extent of their injury. This application goes beyond simply forbidding murder to include preventing harm and ensuring safety, extending the commandment's moral intent into daily life. Similarly, the eighth commandment ("you shall not steal") is applied in Exodus 22:25–27 regarding the regulation of interest on loans, ensuring that someone's financial dealings are just and do not exploit the vulnerable.

Real-World Applications of the Law

The Ten Words are not merely abstract concepts; they have real-world applications that were as relevant in Moses's time as they are in our own. Consider the following applications of the Ten Words through modern parallels:

- Fifth Commandment: "Honor your father and your mother" (Exod. 20:12)

  Moses applies this principle to the family unit and society's foundation. In ancient Israel, the family was the cornerstone of both social and spiritual life. In modern terms, this commandment can be seen in parental rights and family law, which emphasize the protection of family integrity and the responsibility of parents for the care and well-being of children.

Modern Parallel: Family protections and policies that ensure the welfare of children (e.g., child support, education laws) reflect the intent of honoring the foundational authority of parents.

- Sixth Commandment: "You shall not murder" (Exod. 20:13)

  The application of the sixth commandment extends beyond merely prohibiting murder to include ensuring safety and well-being. In Exodus 21:18–19, Moses provides specific guidelines for when an individual causes harm to another. These guidelines protect life and promote responsible behavior within the community.

  Modern Parallel: This law is mirrored in modern safety regulations such as building codes, traffic laws, and workplace safety rules, which all aim to prevent harm and protect individuals from accidents and injury.

- Seventh Commandment: "You shall not commit adultery" (Exod. 20:14)

  In the Book of the Covenant, this commandment emphasizes the sacredness of the marriage relationship. This law preserves trust and fidelity within families and society. In modern contexts, the ethical principle of faithfulness in relationships is still applied to prevent harm to families and communities.

Modern Parallel: Marriage laws that regulate divorce and infidelity, as well as laws against sexual harassment and exploitation, ensure the protection of the marital bond and the dignity of individuals.

- Eighth Commandment: "You shall not steal" (Exod. 20:15)

  Moses applies this to various aspects of life, including property and economic justice. The law establishes guidelines for fair transactions, ensuring that individuals' rights to property are protected.

  Modern Parallel: This is similar to property laws, banking regulations, and anti-theft measures in the modern world such as laws protecting intellectual property, contract law, and the legal consequences of fraud and embezzlement.

- Ninth Commandment: "You shall not give false testimony" (Exod. 20:16)

  Moses applies this commandment in ways that emphasize justice and truthfulness in legal proceedings. False testimony undermines justice and the well-being of individuals and society.

Modern Parallel: This can be compared to laws against perjury and false advertising that protect individuals and society from the harm caused by lies and deception in both legal and commercial matters.

- Tenth Commandment: "You shall not covet" (Exod. 20:17)

  The Tenth Commandment calls attention to the internal desires and attitudes that can lead to covetousness and unjust actions. While this commandment focuses on the heart and the motive behind actions, it also reinforces the importance of contentment and integrity in relationships.

  Modern Parallel: This can be seen in anti-competitive practices in business and consumer protection laws that aim to prevent unfair business practices driven by covetous desires that harm others and distort the market.

The "Then" and the "Now"

The Ten Words serve as an eternal moral foundation, but Moses's application of these words to real-world situations reveals the living nature of the law. While the Ten Words are unchanging, their practical application must be interpreted based on the needs and contexts of the time. The distinction between God's speech in the Ten Words and Moses's applications is key to understanding the dynamic nature of God's moral will.

The law remains relevant today, just as it was when Moses applied it to the Israelites who would enter the Promised Land. As we move forward in our study, we will explore how the Sermon on the Mount and the teachings of Jesus demonstrate that the true intent of the Ten Words is not just about external behavior but about an internal transformation that fulfills the true intent of God's law.

Conclusion

In this chapter, we've explored the distinction between God's direct speech in the Ten Words and Moses's applications of those words to Israel's real-life context. The Ten Words provide the moral law, and Moses's applications illustrate how these principles take shape in the practical life of God's people. By understanding the eternal nature of God's law and its contextual applications, we can see how the moral intent behind the Ten Words continues to guide our lives today. The real-world applications of the law, illustrated through modern parallels, remind us that God's moral law is as relevant now as it was when it was first spoken.

Study Guide for Chapter 3

God's Direct Speech and Applied Law

Summary:

God's Ten Words are universal moral law; Moses' applications illustrate timeless principles in historical context.

Discussion Questions:

1. Why does it matter that the Ten Words were spoken directly by God?

2. How does distinguishing principles from applications help modern believers?

3. What modern examples parallel Moses' applications of the Law?

Application:

Identify a moral principle and describe a modern application.

Scripture Reflection: Exodus 20

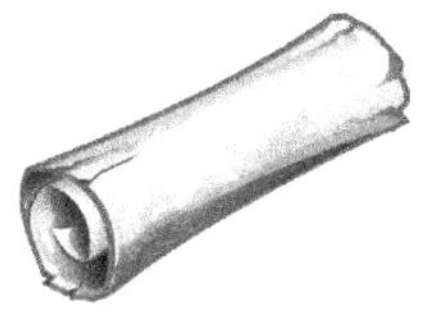

Chapter 4:

THE "THEN" AND THE "NOW": THE UNIQUENESS OF GOD'S SPEECH AND THE APPLICATION OF THE LAW (COMMANDS 1-4)

God Speaks Directly: The First Four Commandments

The first set of the Ten Words—commands 1–4—relates directly to humanity's relationship with God. These laws are foundational to understanding not only the structure of the Decalogue but also the eternal moral law that governs the interaction between the Creator and His people.

The first commandment, "You shall have no other gods before me," establishes the priority of God. It insists that nothing in the created world should be given a place that rivals the Creator Himself. This commandment is universal, asserting that God alone is worthy of worship and allegiance.

The second commandment prohibits the making of graven images or idols, emphasizing that our worship must be spiritual, not material. The essence of worship is not found in objects or representations but in the reverence and submission to God's immensity and sovereignty.

The third commandment, "You shall not misuse the name of the Lord your God," calls God's people to a proper reverence for His name, which represents His character and authority. To use God's name carelessly or falsely is to diminish His holiness and authority over all creation.

The fourth commandment, "Remember the Sabbath day by keeping it holy," serves as a reminder that God, having created the world, also provides for the rest and flourishing of His people. The Sabbath is not just a day of physical rest but a day of spiritual renewal, a time to acknowledge the Creator's provision and sovereignty over time itself.

These first four commandments underscore the centrality of God in all aspects of life, establishing a covenantal relationship with His people that is exclusive, reverent, and sanctified.

Application in the Hebrew Bible

In the Pentateuch, these commandments are foundational to Israel's identity as a covenant people. The first commandment is reiterated in various forms such as in Deuteronomy 6:4 where the Shema proclaims, "Hear, O Israel: The Lord our God, the Lord is one." This declaration affirms the monotheism central to Israel's worship and understanding of God.

The second commandment's prohibition of idols is illustrated in Exodus 32 where the people's worship of the golden calf is condemned as a direct violation of God's will. Moses destroys the idol to show that nothing should take the place of God's transcendent presence.

The third commandment is linked to God's holiness and the proper use of His name, as seen in passages such as Leviticus 19:12 that warns against swearing falsely by God's name. This reflects the respect and reverence that the Hebrew Scriptures demand in regard to God's character.

The fourth commandment finds application in Exodus 16 where the Israelites are instructed to observe the Sabbath and refrain from gathering manna on the seventh day. It highlights the importance of God's provision and the rhythms of rest He ordained for His people.

Study Guide for Chapter 4

The "Then" and the "Now": The Uniqueness of God's Speech and the Application of the Law (Commands 1–4)

Summary:

These commandments govern humanity's relationship to God, emphasizing exclusive worship, reverence, and sabbath trust.

Discussion Questions:

1. How does each of the first four commandments shape worship?

2. Why is sabbath ultimately about trust?

3. Where do modern Christians face temptations toward idolatry?

Application:

Practice a sabbath-oriented rhythm this week.

Scripture Reflection: Deuteronomy 6:4

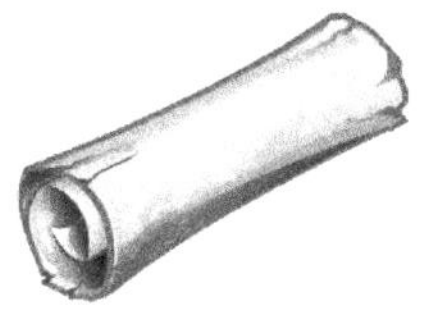

Chapter 5:
THE "THEN" AND THE "NOW": THE UNIQUENESS OF GOD'S SPEECH AND THE APPLICATION OF THE LAW (COMMANDS 5-10)

Responsibilities to One Another: The Last Six Commandments

The second set of commandments—commands 5–10—focuses on our relationships with one another and the moral order that governs human society. These laws are practical applications of the moral law in daily life, dealing with issues of justice, relationships, and integrity.

The fifth commandment, "Honor your father and your mother," is the first commandment with a promise, tied to the well-being and flourishing of society. This commandment reflects the importance of family structure and respect for authority within the household as the foundation for a stable society.

The sixth commandment, "You shall not murder," emphasizes the sanctity of human life and calls for the protection of the innocent. The broader application of this commandment extends to issues of justice, care for the vulnerable, and the promotion of peace within the community.

The seventh commandment, "You shall not commit adultery," highlights the importance of faithfulness in marriage and the protection of sexual integrity. It guards against covetousness and the exploitation of all relationships, ensuring that personal commitments are honored and society remains orderly.

The eighth commandment, "You shall not steal," reflects the right to private property and the importance of justice in all economic transactions. It safeguards the integrity of personal property and calls for fairness in dealings with others.

The ninth commandment, "You shall not give false testimony against your neighbor," emphasizes the importance of truthfulness in legal proceedings and personal relations. It calls for the protection of reputations and the preservation of justice in society.

The tenth commandment, "You shall not covet," addresses the desires of the heart, calling for contentment and the prevention of envy and covetousness. This commandment underscores the importance of inner purity and the guarding of desires that lead to unjust actions.

Application in the Hebrew Bible

These commandments are applied throughout the Pentateuch and Israel's social life. For instance, the fifth commandment of honoring parents is reiterated in Deuteronomy 21:18–21 where the disobedient son is dealt with severely, emphasizing the importance of family order in society.

The sixth commandment, which prohibits murder, is applied in Exodus 21:12–14 where the law addresses the intentional and unintentional taking of life, outlining the consequences for manslaughter.

The seventh commandment is demonstrated in the laws about marital fidelity in Leviticus 20:10 where adultery is punished severely, underscoring the importance of sexual integrity.

The eighth commandment finds application in Exodus 22:1–9 where the principles of restitution for stolen goods are laid out, promoting justice and fairness in Israel's society.

The ninth commandment is reflected in the prohibition of false testimony in Exodus 23:1–3, which aims to ensure justice in legal matters and prevent harm to an individual's reputation.

Finally, the tenth commandment is implicitly reflected in the warnings against covetousness in Deuteronomy 5:21 where the people are warned not to covet the belongings of their neighbors, emphasizing that inward desires can lead to sinful actions.

Conclusion

The Ten Words provide a moral framework for understanding our relationship with God and one another. By examining the broader moral applications of each commandment through biblical passages, we see how these laws are not merely rules but reflect God's character and His intent for human flourishing. The Decalogue is not just a list of commands but a covenantal framework that shapes how we live in community with God and with each other. As we continue to explore the moral law in the Hebrew Bible, we see that the Ten Words remain relevant today, guiding us toward a life that reflects justice, mercy, and holiness.

Study Guide for Chapter 5

The "Then" and the "Now": The Uniqueness of God's Speech and the Application of the Law (Commands 5–10)

Summary:

These commandments shape social relationships—family, life, fidelity, property, speech, and contentment.

Discussion Questions:

1. Which of these commands most challenges contemporary culture?

2. Why does the Decalogue end with a command about desire?

3. How do these commands form a just society?

Application:

Choose one command and identify one practical way to embody it today.

Scripture Reflection: Exodus 20:12–17

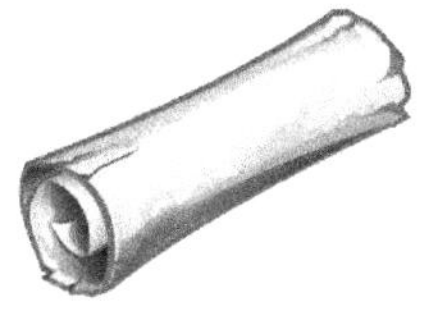

Chapter 6:

WISDOM LITERATURE: THE PRACTICAL APPLICATION OF THE LAW IN DAILY LIFE

The Wisdom Literature of the Old Testament— books such as Proverbs, Ecclesiastes, Psalms and Job—provides a unique lens through which we can understand the practical application of God's moral law. These books serve as a bridge between the moral laws presented in the Decalogue and the realities of daily living. Wisdom Literature is not just theoretical but is deeply practical, showing how God's principles shape the believer's daily life.

The moral law, as expressed in the Ten Commandments, is comprehensive. It covers everything from our relationship to God to our relationships with others. Wisdom Literature takes these high moral principles and applies them to the specific situations we face in our everyday lives. This practical wisdom is not just an intellectual pursuit but is meant to lead to right action, helping individuals align their lives with God's design for human flourishing.

Wisdom: Not Just Spiritual, but Practical Excellence

Wisdom, as exemplified in the book of Proverbs and in the life of Solomon, is not confined to spiritual matters alone; it encompasses the skillful and thoughtful application of knowledge in every area of life. When the Queen of Sheba visited Solomon, she was overwhelmed by the order and excellence of his kingdom, remarking that she was literally without breath (1 Kings 10:4–5). This awe was not simply because of Solomon's spiritual insight but because everything he did was done with wisdom—from his governance and architecture to his stewardship of resources. Wisdom is about doing all things well. This theme is further reinforced in the New Testament where Jesus is described as growing in wisdom and stature before both God and man (Luke 2:40). The culmination of Jesus's wisdom is revealed in Mark 7:37 where the people marveled, saying, "He has done everything well." Wisdom, then, is a holistic trait that leads to excellence in all things—in relationships, work, speech, and even in the smallest details of daily life.

The Role of Wisdom Literature in Understanding the Law

The Wisdom Literature emphasizes that true wisdom begins with a fear of the Lord (Prov. 1:7; Eccles. 12:13). Moral law is the foundation for this wisdom. Without it, there is no true wisdom. However, Wisdom Literature goes beyond the rules of the Ten Commandments, offering guidance on how to live out those rules in a broken world.

While the Decalogue offers a moral foundation, Wisdom Literature helps us apply those moral principles in the complexities of life. For example, Proverbs shows us how to live wisely in community, how to handle money, and how to speak truthfully. Job and Ecclesiastes wrestle with the complexities of suffering and the seeming injustices of life, providing wisdom for living in a world where things do not always go as they should.

The moral law calls for specific behaviors such as honoring parents, keeping the Sabbath, and not lying. Wisdom Literature takes these commands and shows how to embody them in every circumstance. It explains how God's moral law, far from being a set of rigid, outdated rules, is a living guide that leads to wisdom and flourishing in daily life.

The Relationship Between the Decalogue and Wisdom Literature

The connection between the Ten Commandments and Wisdom Literature is profound. Both are concerned with the same goal: to live rightly in relationship to God and others.

The Decalogue sets the standard for moral living, while Wisdom Literature shows us how to live out these standards in practical, daily ways. For example, look at the following comparisons.

The first commandment, which calls for exclusive loyalty to God, is echoed in the Wisdom Literature's call to avoid idolatry and to seek wisdom above all else (Prov. 3:5–6).

The second commandment, which forbids the making of idols, finds its counterpart in Proverbs 4:23 where we are told to guard our hearts because from them flow the issues of life. This command implies that idolatry is not just about images of stone or wood but involves anything we elevate above God in our hearts.

The sixth commandment, which prohibits murder, aligns with Wisdom Literature's teachings on the sanctity of life and the importance of loving others. Proverbs 14:21 states, "It is a sin to despise one's neighbor, but blessed is the one who is kind to the needy."

The ninth commandment, which forbids bearing false witness, is echoed throughout Proverbs where truthfulness is presented as a virtue to be pursued in every area of life. Proverbs 12:22 says, "The Lord detests lying lips, but he delights in people who are trustworthy."

Wisdom Literature doesn't just restate the Ten Commandments; it expands and applies these laws to every area of life, helping believers embody God's law in the full range of their relationships, work, and even internal lives.

Wisdom for Relationships

One of the most compelling ways Wisdom Literature applies God's moral law is in the area of relationships. Whether it is our relationship with family members, friends, or coworkers, Wisdom Literature provides a framework for living in harmony with others.

Proverbs emphasizes the importance of honoring parents (Prov. 1:8), speaking truthfully (Prov. 12:17), and seeking justice (Prov. 21:15). These principles help shape a society where individuals treat each other with respect, kindness, and fairness.

Job and Ecclesiastes provide a more sobering outlook on life, reminding us that the world is broken and unpredictable, but we can still live wisely by trusting in God's sovereignty. Job teaches us about integrity in suffering, while Ecclesiastes encourages us to fear God and enjoy life's simple pleasures while acknowledging the limits of human understanding.

Wisdom for Work and Wealth

Wisdom Literature also addresses the realities of work and wealth, areas that the Decalogue does not go into detail about but that are essential to daily living. Proverbs offers practical advice for living wisely in the workplace, such as working diligently (Prov. 10:4), being honest in business (Prov. 11:1), and practicing generosity (Prov. 19:17).

Proverbs also teaches that money is not the ultimate goal

in life. Proverbs 23:4–5 warns against overworking for wealth and reminds us that true contentment comes not from material possessions but from trusting in God.

The Role of Wisdom in Spiritual Maturity

At its core, wisdom in the Old Testament is about growing in spiritual maturity. As the Proverbs repeatedly emphasize, the fear of the Lord is the beginning of wisdom (Prov. 9:10). This is not mere intellectual knowledge but a heartfelt reverence for God that leads to transformation.

Wisdom Literature teaches that the moral law is not about following a set of rules for their own sake but about living in right relationship with God, others, and the world He has made. The moral commands of the Decalogue help shape a wise heart, one that seeks justice, mercy, and humility in every area of life.

Conclusion

Wisdom Literature takes the moral law and applies it to the realities of everyday life. It shows how to live wisely in relationships, work, and the pursuit of wealth. By doing so, it helps us see how the Ten Commandments are not outdated rules but eternal principles that lead to godly living and human flourishing.

As we seek to live according to God's law, Wisdom Literature teaches us that wisdom is not just knowledge but the practical application of God's will in the world. The Decalogue is the foundation, but Wisdom Literature shows us how to build our lives on that foundation in a way that honors God and serves the good of others.

Study Guide for Chapter 6

Wisdom Literature:
The Practical Application of the Law in Daily Life

Summary:
Wisdom is skillful obedience—practically applying God's Law to all of life.

Discussion Questions:

1. How does Proverbs apply the Decalogue to daily life?

2. What do Job and Ecclesiastes teach about wisdom amid suffering?

3. Why is excellence a spiritual virtue?

Application:

Apply one principle from Proverbs to a current challenge.

Scripture Reflection: Proverbs 1:7

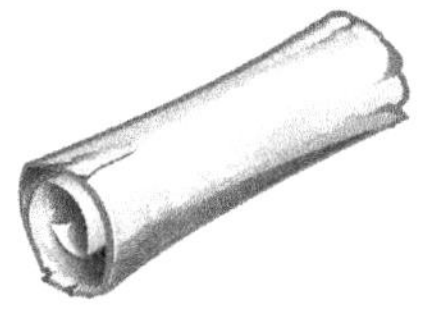

Chapter 7: THE LAW IN THE PSALMS: AN INTEGRAL FOUNDATION FOR WORSHIP

The Psalms are often considered the heart of Israel's worship and prayer. These sacred songs, poems, and prayers express a deep reverence for God, a longing for justice, and an intimate relationship with the Creator. What is striking about the Psalms is their consistent foundation in the law. Throughout the Psalms, God's moral law is not only mentioned but is also integral to the way the psalmists understand their relationship with God and His expectations for their lives.

While the Pentateuch lays out God's moral law in a systematic way, the Psalms bring that law into the context of lived experience—showing how the law of God is not an abstract set of rules but a living reality that shapes the worshiper's heart, actions, and spiritual life. The Psalms express the joy of those who live in accordance with God's law, the anguish of those who have violated it, and the hope for redemption when the law is broken.

The Law as the Foundation of Worship

The law is not just a set of commands in the Psalms; it is seen as a guide for worship and spiritual formation. The psalmists regularly affirm that their delight and meditation are in God's law. Psalm 1, for example, describes the blessed person as one who delights in the law of the Lord and meditates on it day and night. This love for God's law is not a begrudging obedience but a joyful commitment to living in accordance with God's will.

In Psalm 119, the longest psalm in the Bible, the law of the Lord is mentioned several dozen times, and it is praised for its role in guiding the faithful. The psalmist calls the law a lamp to his feet and a light to his path (Ps. 119:105). The law gives direction, wisdom, and understanding to the believer. It is more than mere legal instruction; it is the basis for knowing God and living rightly in His world.

The law's centrality to worship in the Psalms suggests that right worship is inextricably linked to right living. The psalmists did not see the law as a barrier to communion with God but as a means to express their love and devotion to Him. By aligning their lives with God's commands, they could enter His presence with confidence and joy.

The Law as Revealing God's Character

For the psalmists, the law was a revelation of God's character. The moral law reflects God's holiness, justice, mercy, and faithfulness. Through His law, God reveals His desires for the world; namely, that justice be upheld, truth be spoken, and love be demonstrated toward others.

Psalm 11:7 says, "For the Lord is righteous; he loves justice; the upright will see his face." The law reveals the righteousness of God and points the way for humans to reflect that righteousness in their own lives.

Psalm 33:5 states, "The Lord loves righteousness and justice; the earth is full of his unfailing love." The law helps Israel understand that God's justice is not separate from His love; they are interwoven. God's law calls His people to love justice and righteousness, as He does.

In the Psalms, obedience to God's law is often linked to the blessing of His presence. Psalm 19:7–8 proclaims, "The law of the Lord is perfect, refreshing the soul, . . . making wise the simple . . . giving joy to the heart." These verses capture the psalmist's sense that God's law is not burdensome but is a gift that reveals His goodness and grace.

The Law and Human Suffering

The Psalms also demonstrate how the law provides comfort in times of suffering. The law is not just a guide for good living; it is a source of hope when things go wrong. The psalmists often cry out to God for deliverance and seek solace in the fact that God's Word, which includes His law, is a secure refuge in times of distress.

In Psalm 119:67, the psalmist says, "Before I was afflicted I went astray, but now I obey your word." This verse points to the corrective role of God's law—how it guides us back to the right path in times of failure and suffering. The psalmist finds comfort not in the absence of pain but in the presence of a faithful God who will guide him through suffering according to His good law.

Additionally, Psalm 94:12–13 declares, "Blessed is the one you discipline, Lord, the one you teach from your law; you grant them relief from days of trouble." The law becomes a source of peace even in times of trouble as the faithful trust in God's justice and sovereignty.

The Law and Hope for Redemption

While the law is foundational for living according to God's will, the Psalms also express the need for redemption when the law is broken. In many of the psalms, the psalmists acknowledge their sin and seek forgiveness and restoration. Psalm 51, a classic example, shows how the psalmist, King David, appeals to God's mercy, asking for a clean heart and a right spirit after his sin with Bathsheba. The law condemns sin, but the psalmist's cry for mercy reveals the hope of forgiveness and the restoration of a relationship with God.

Psalm 103:10–12 reflects this beautifully: "He does not

treat us as our sins deserve or repay us according to our iniquities. For as high as the heavens are above the earth, so great is his love for those who fear him; as far as the east is from the west, so far has he removed our transgressions from us." This redemption is possible because of God's covenant love, and the law reveals the need for God's grace and forgiveness.

Conclusion

The Psalms underscore the vital role of God's law in the life of the believer. Far from being a set of restrictive rules, the law is seen as life-giving and integral to the worship of the living God. Through the Psalms, we see that the law is a tool for worship, a revelation of God's character, a guide in times of suffering, and a path to redemption.

The Psalms reflect the joy and peace found in aligning your life with God's moral law. In doing so, they echo the overarching message of the Decalogue, that God's law is good, and it leads to human flourishing as we live in relationship with the Creator. In the Psalms, the moral law is not merely an ancient set of rules but a living expression of God's will for the believer's life today.

Study Guide for Chapter 7

The Law in the Psalms: An Integral Foundation for Worship

Summary:

The Psalms reveal the Law as essential to worship, spiritual formation, and hope.

Discussion Questions:

1. Why do the psalmists delight in the Law?

2. How does the Law comfort in suffering?

3. How does the Law reveal God's character?

Application:

Meditate on a passage from Psalm 119 this week.

Scripture Reflection: Psalm 1

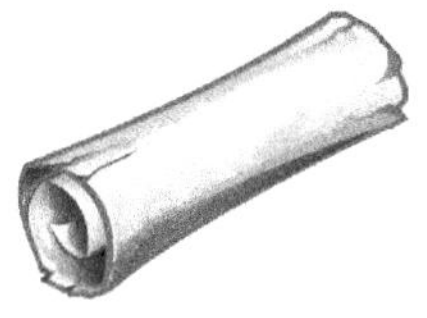

Chapter 8:

PROVERBS - THE SETTLED APPLICATION OF GOD'S LAW IN DAILY LIFE

Introduction: From Decalogue to Daily Wisdom

The Book of Proverbs stands as a vivid representation of how the moral imperatives of the Decalogue (the Ten Commandments) are woven into the fabric of everyday life. In Deuteronomy, Moses exhorted Israel to obey God's law, noting that adherence to these commands would display their wisdom to the nations. Proverbs picks up this theme, transforming the abstract principles of the Decalogue into practical, everyday wisdom that guides how we should live in various situations, from relationships to work and beyond.

The essence of Proverbs is encapsulated in its view that wisdom is the settled application of the law of God to daily life. Unlike abstract theories or ideals, wisdom in Proverbs is highly practical, offering counsel on issues such as speech, family life, honesty, and justice. The Proverbs aren't mere moral platitudes; they are the living out of God's moral law shown in the day-to-day decisions and character of the believer.

Wisdom's Worldview: God-View, Life-View, Way of Life

At the heart of Proverbs lies a comprehensive worldview that integrates three central aspects: a view of God (God-View), a view of life (Life-View), and a way of life (Way of Life).

> *View of God (God-View):* Proverbs begins with the fundamental assumption that wisdom comes from reverence for God. "The fear of the Lord is the beginning of wisdom" (Prov. 9:10). This God-centered worldview forms the foundation for all the other wisdom that Proverbs imparts. The wise person acknowledges God's authority in all things, recognizing that His ways lead to life, and His commands are the path to fulfillment.
>
> *View of Life (Life-View):* Proverbs teaches that life is not random but follows a moral order established by God. This order operates according to righteousness, justice, and truth, and all decisions—whether in family, work, or community—should align with these principles. Proverbs recognizes that life is complex and sometimes difficult but insists that those who follow God's

wisdom will experience peace and blessing. Proverbs emphasizes that a life well-lived is one that adheres to these moral principles.

Way of Life (Way of Life): The practical application of this worldview leads to the way of life prescribed in Proverbs. The way of wisdom is not merely theoretical or abstract but involves real, concrete decisions made daily. Proverbs shows how wisdom applies to ordinary circumstances—how to speak, how to work, how to relate to others, and how to lead a life marked by integrity, fairness, and justice. It highlights two distinct paths: the way of the wise who follow God's commands, and the way of the fool who rejects them.

Structure of the Book of Proverbs

Proverbs is divided into sections, each offering a different perspective on how wisdom should be applied:

Proverbs 1–9: Wisdom's Call and Parental Instruction: These chapters serve as an introduction to the whole book, presenting wisdom as a personified figure calling out to all who will listen. This section emphasizes the importance of fearing God, following parental instruction, and avoiding the dangers of folly. It also introduces the concept that wisdom leads to life and peace, while folly leads to destruction.

Proverbs 10–24: The Proverbs of Solomon (Short Sayings): These chapters contain the classic one- or two-line proverbs that have made the book famous. They offer practical advice on a wide range of topics: relationships, speech, business, and personal character. Each proverb reflects the application of God's law to real-life situations, presenting wisdom in a highly accessible format.

Proverbs 25–29: Additional Sayings of Solomon: These proverbs were compiled by the men of King Hezekiah, offering further insights into wisdom and its application. While these proverbs follow a similar structure to those found earlier, they offer a deeper exploration of topics such as leadership, righteousness, and community life.

Proverbs 30–31: The Words of Agur and King Lemuel and the Virtuous Woman: The final chapters of Proverbs contain sayings that focus on the limitations of human wisdom (Agur) and the qualities of a wise and virtuous woman (the famous Proverbs 31 woman). Agur's prayer for wisdom reflects the first and third commandments, showing that true wisdom comes from God alone. The Proverbs 31 woman embodies a life of godly wisdom, living out the principles of the Decalogue in every aspect of her daily life.

Proverbs and the Ten Commandments

One of the key insights of Proverbs is that wisdom is not divorced from morality; it is a living embodiment of God's law in action. Throughout the book, the principles of the Ten Commandments are applied to specific situations, demonstrating how the believer can live out the law in practical ways. Each of the Ten Commandments finds concrete expression in the teachings of Proverbs.

Honor God (First Through Fourth Commandments): Throughout Proverbs, there is a constant emphasis on the fear of the Lord as the beginning of wisdom. From acknowledging God's sovereignty to guarding against idolatry and keeping the Sabbath, Proverbs teaches that true wisdom begins with honoring God in every area of life.

Honor Parents (Fifth Commandment): Proverbs repeatedly stresses the importance of honoring our parents, particularly through listening to their wisdom and following their instruction. This foundational principle is extended to a broader respect for authority and wise counsel.

Respect Life (Sixth Commandment): Proverbs upholds the sanctity of life, teaching that violence, anger, and hatred are to be avoided. The book encourages a peaceful, life-affirming way of living that seeks reconciliation and fosters respect for others.

Faithfulness and Purity (Seventh Commandment): Adultery is strongly condemned in Proverbs, with numerous warnings about the dangers of sexual immorality. The book highlights the importance of faithfulness in marriage and the integrity of relationships, emphasizing the value of purity in thought and deed.

Integrity and Work Ethic (Eighth Commandment): Proverbs underscores the importance of honesty and hard work. It teaches that diligence leads to prosperity, while laziness and dishonesty lead to ruin. The book also encourages generosity, particularly toward the poor, as an outworking of the eighth commandment.

Speaking Truth (Ninth Commandment): Proverbs calls for truthfulness in speech, warning against lies, gossip, and deceit. The book places a high value on honesty and integrity, showing that a wise person speaks the truth in love while the fool spreads lies and misinformation.

Contentment and Generosity (Tenth Commandment): Proverbs teaches contentment with our portion, warning against covetousness and envy. The book encourages generosity, especially toward the poor, and warns that greed leads to ruin. Wisdom is presented as the antidote to covetous desires, leading to a life of peace and satisfaction.

Living Wisdom: Law Applied to Relationships and Character

Proverbs is not just a collection of wise sayings but a guide to living out the moral principles of the Ten Commandments in every area of life. The book teaches that wisdom is not merely about knowing what is right but living it out in practical ways. It provides wisdom for relationships, guiding how we should treat family, friends, and neighbors in line with God's commands—honoring parents, being faithful in marriage, speaking truth, and seeking justice. It also offers wisdom for work and wealth, applying commandments about stealing and coveting into principles of diligent labor, fair business practices, and generosity to the poor.

In every sphere, Proverbs shows that God's law is not an archaic list of rules but a living guide to what is good, right, and just. The book's very premise—that fearing God leads to wisdom—indicates that ethical living (keeping God's law) and practical living (making wise choices) are one and the same.

Conclusion: Proverbs as a Bridge from Law to Life

By examining Proverbs as the settled application of God's law to daily life, we see that the book serves as a practical bridge between the revelation of God's will and the responsive living of God's people. Proverbs demonstrates that the Ten Commandments are not burdensome relics but eternal principles that lead to godly living and human flourishing. Through its teachings, Proverbs equips believers to internalize God's law and let it shape their character and choices, moving from knowing God's commandments to doing them in everyday life. The Proverbs 31 woman exemplifies this perfectly, showing that wisdom is a reflection of God's law in action. Through wisdom, we learn to walk in God's truth and live a life that honors Him.

Study Guide for Chapter 8

Proverbs – The Settled Application of God's Law in Daily Life

Summary:

Proverbs shows the Decalogue lived out through a God-view, Life-view, and Way-of-life.

Discussion Questions:

1. What distinguishes the way of the wise from the way of the fool?

2. How does Proverbs connect wisdom and moral obedience?

3. Which proverb most clearly echoes the Ten Commandments?

Application:

Memorize a proverb that applies to your current season.

Scripture Reflection: Proverbs 3:5–6

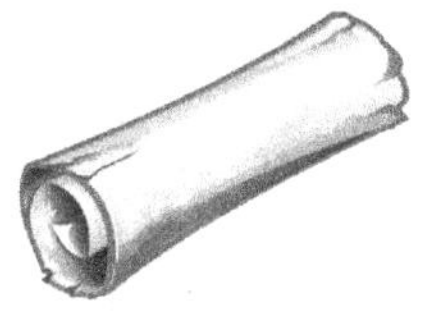

Chapter 9:

THE PROVERBS 31 WOMAN - A LIFE OF COVENANT FAITHFULNESS

Introduction: The Proverbs 31 Woman as the Embodiment of Wisdom

Proverbs 31 presents the wise woman as a living, breathing example of the application of God's law in daily life. She is the culmination of the wisdom imparted throughout the entire book of Proverbs. Her life exemplifies a deep, internalized wisdom, rooted in the fear of the Lord and lived out in her roles as a wife, mother, and member of the community. Proverbs 31 is not just a description of a virtuous woman; it is a portrait of covenant faithfulness, illustrating how a woman's actions and choices reflect the moral and ethical teachings of the Ten Commandments.

As we examine the Proverbs 31 woman, we see how each of the Ten Commandments is beautifully embodied in her character and conduct. In this chapter, we will explore how she applies these commandments in her relationships, work, speech, and service to others. In doing so, the Proverbs 31 woman becomes a model for all believers—both men and women—showing us what it means to live faithfully under God's law.

The Fear of the Lord: The Foundation of Wisdom

The key to understanding the Proverbs 31 woman is her deep reverence for God. Proverbs 31:30 tells us, "Charm is deceptive, and beauty is fleeting; but a woman who fears the Lord is to be praised." Her wisdom begins with the fear of the Lord, which is the foundational principle of all biblical wisdom. As we have seen throughout the book of Proverbs, wisdom is not just an intellectual exercise but a moral and spiritual one. The Proverbs 31 woman's life is marked by her acknowledgment of God's sovereignty, and this reverence shapes her priorities, her actions, and her relationships.

The fear of the Lord leads her to honor and obey God in all aspects of her life. Whether she is managing her household, engaging in work, or serving her community, she does so with a deep sense of God's presence and authority. Her wisdom is not her own; it flows from her relationship with the Lord and her willingness to live in accordance with His commands.

Honoring God (First Through Fourth Commandments): A Life Devoted to Worship and Service

The Proverbs 31 woman honors God in all she does. This is evident not only in her reverence for the Lord but in her practical application of His law. As we have seen in the analysis of Proverbs, honoring God involves not just worship but a life that reflects His holiness and justice. The Proverbs 31 woman's fear of the Lord is the basis of her wisdom, and everything she does flows from this foundation.

First Commandment (no other gods before me): The Proverbs 31 woman shows her exclusive devotion to God. She lives a life that is centered on Him, with no competing idols or distractions. Her work, her family, and her service all point to God's glory, showing that for her, there is no other God but the Lord.

Second Commandment (no idols): The woman's faithfulness to God means she is not swayed by the allure of false gods or the idolatry of materialism. Her trust is in the Lord's provision, and her heart is set on serving Him with undivided devotion. Proverbs 31:30 reminds us that her beauty is not external but comes from her fear of the Lord, indicating that her inner devotion to God is her true source of value.

Third Commandment (honor God's name): She honors God's name by living a life of integrity. Her speech and actions reflect God's holiness, showing respect for His name in all things. As we saw in the earlier chapters of Proverbs, wisdom is characterized by truthfulness and a commitment to uphold the reputation of the Lord in every area of life.

Fourth Commandment (honor the Sabbath): While the Sabbath is not explicitly mentioned in Proverbs 31, the principles of rest and trust in God's provision are evident in the woman's life. She works diligently but also ensures that her household is well-managed and that others are cared for, reflecting the balance of work and rest that the Sabbath commandment embodies. Her ability to rest in God's provision allows her to focus on what truly matters: God, family, and community.

Honor Parents (Fifth Commandment): The Proverbs 31 Woman as a Mother and Wife

The Proverbs 31 woman embodies the fifth commandment through her dedication to her family and her role as a wife and mother. Proverbs 31:28 states, "Her children arise and call her blessed; her husband also, and he praises her." Her actions as a mother and wife are a direct reflection of her respect for the authority of her husband and her role in nurturing and guiding her children.

Her children call her blessed because she has taught them wisdom, character, and the fear of the Lord. She is a model of godly living, and her influence on her children helps them grow in the way of wisdom. As a wife, she respects her husband

and works alongside him to manage the household. Their relationship is built on mutual respect, love, and trust, all of which stem from her adherence to God's design for marriage and family.

Respect Life (Sixth Commandment): The Proverbs 31 Woman as a Peacemaker

The Proverbs 31 woman demonstrates respect for life through her actions of kindness, generosity, and care for others. Proverbs 31:20 states, "She opens her arms to the poor and extends her hands to the needy." In caring for those in need, she affirms the sanctity of life, demonstrating that life is valuable in all its forms, whether in the home or among the poor and marginalized.

By promoting peace, harmony, and care for others, the Proverbs 31 woman reflects the sixth commandment's call to preserve and respect life. Her actions are not motivated by selfishness or violence but by a desire to contribute to the well-being of those around her, showing that true wisdom values life and works to protect and nurture it.

Faithfulness and Purity (Seventh Commandment): A Model of Marital Faithfulness

Faithfulness in marriage is a cornerstone of the Proverbs 31 woman's life. Proverbs 31:11–12 states, "Her husband has full confidence in her and lacks nothing of value. She brings him good, not harm, all the days of her life." She is a model of fidelity, commitment, and purity in her marriage. Her faithfulness to her husband reflects her integrity in all aspects of her life.

The Proverbs 31 woman exemplifies the application of the seventh commandment by remaining loyal to her husband and keeping her marriage relationship pure. She avoids all forms of immorality and demonstrates integrity in her sexual and relational commitments. Her faithfulness extends beyond her marriage to include all relationships, showing that the seventh commandment's principle of fidelity applies to all areas of life, not just marriage.

Integrity and Work Ethic (Eighth Commandment): The Proverbs 31 Woman's Diligence

The Proverbs 31 woman is an industrious worker who manages her household and engages in business with integrity. Proverbs 31:13 and 16 describe her work ethic, noting that "she selects wool and flax and works with eager hands . . . . She considers a field and buys it; out of her earnings she plants a vineyard." Her diligence and resourcefulness reflect the eighth commandment, which calls for honest work and the respectful handling of resources.

She does not steal or take what is not hers; rather, she works hard and is diligent in managing her affairs. Her work is not motivated by selfishness or greed but by a desire to provide for her family and to bless others. Her efforts are a reflection of God's provision, and she uses her resources to help others, thereby fulfilling the eighth commandment by using what she has for the good of her family and the wider community.

Speaking Truth (Ninth Commandment): A Life of Integrity and Honesty

The Proverbs 31 woman is characterized by her wise and truthful speech. Proverbs 31:26 states, "She speaks with wisdom, and faithful instruction is on her tongue." Her words reflect the ninth commandment, which calls for truth and honesty. The Proverbs 31 woman speaks truthfully, encourages others, and uses her speech to bring about good in the world.

She is not known for gossip, slander, or falsehood but for her wisdom and integrity. Her speech is an embodiment of the ninth commandment as she upholds truth in all her interactions, both in her home and in the community. By speaking truth and kindness, she builds trust and fosters strong, healthy relationships.

Contentment and Generosity (Tenth Commandment): A Heart Free from Covetousness

The Proverbs 31 woman exemplifies contentment with what she has and generosity to others. Proverbs 31:20 states, "She opens her arms to the poor and extends her hands to the needy." She is content with her lot in life and does not covet what others have. Instead, she uses her resources to bless others, reflecting the tenth commandment's call to avoid covetousness.

She does not accumulate wealth for its own sake but seeks to use it for the good of others. Her generosity is a reflection of her contentment in the provision of God, and her ability to live without envy or greed illustrates the application of the tenth commandment in her life.

Conclusion: The Proverbs 31 Woman as a Picture of Covenant Faithfulness

The Proverbs 31 woman is a living example of covenant faithfulness. She embodies the application of the Ten Commandments in her daily life, demonstrating how wisdom and godliness are lived out through the commandments in practical ways. Her life is a testimony to the fact that the commandments are not just rules to follow but a framework for living a flourishing, godly life.

She honors God in all her actions, respects authority, values life, remains faithful in marriage, works diligently, speaks truthfully, and practices contentment and generosity. In every aspect of her life, she reflects the principles of God's law, showing how a life devoted to wisdom leads to a flourishing life in harmony with God's order. The Proverbs 31 woman stands as a model for all believers, teaching us how to live in accordance with God's law in every area of life.

Study Guide for Chapter 9

The Proverbs 31 Woman – A Life of Covenant Faithfulness

Summary:

A portrait of covenant faithfulness, she embodies the Ten Commandments in her life and relationships.

Discussion Questions:

1. How does fear of the Lord shape her identity?

2. Which commandment is most clearly embodied in her character?

3. What does her example reveal about everyday holiness?

Application:

Identify one virtue from this chapter to cultivate.

Scripture Reflection: Proverbs 31:30

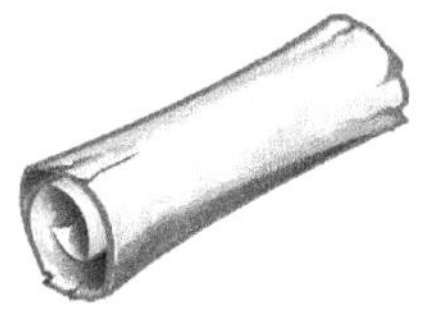

Chapter 10:

THE BOOK OF LAMENTATIONS: GOD'S FAITHFULNESS AMIDST JUDGMENT

Introduction

The Book of Lamentations, a poignant reflection of Israel's grief over the fall of Jerusalem, stands as a literary and theological masterpiece. Often viewed through the lens of mourning and sorrow, it offers profound insights into the nature of God's faithfulness. At its core, Lamentations is a lament for the destruction of Jerusalem in 586 BC, a result of the nation's unfaithfulness to God. Written by the prophet Jeremiah, the book chronicles the pain of exile, the ruins of the city, and the trauma experienced by the people of Israel. However, amid this sorrow, Lamentations 3 particularly stands out, proclaiming

God's faithfulness in the face of divine judgment. This chapter explores that paradox—that God's faithfulness is demonstrated even in His execution of judgment—and highlights how this faithfulness relates to the blessings and curses found in Deuteronomy 28.

Historical Context: The Fall of Jerusalem

The backdrop of Lamentations is the destruction of Jerusalem by the Babylonians under King Nebuchadnezzar. This moment in Israel's history was one of complete devastation. The city was razed, the Temple—the heart of Israel's worship—was destroyed, and the nation was scattered in exile. This calamity fulfilled the covenantal promises of Deuteronomy 28 where God warned Israel of the consequences of disobedience: destruction, disease, exile, and social chaos. Yet amid this profound tragedy, the book of Lamentations proclaims that God is faithful, even in His judgment.

The Paradox of Faithfulness in Judgment

In Lamentations 3, the prophet presents a stark paradox: God's faithfulness is seen even in His judgment. The hymn of faithfulness found in Lamentations 3:22–23 ("Great Is Thy Faithfulness") arises from the recognition that Israel, in its disobedience, has received the consequences promised in the covenant. Jeremiah is not denying the tragedy; he is acknowledging that the pain is the result of God's justice. In this sense, the faithfulness of God is not just seen in restoration but also in the consistency with which He upholds His covenant, fulfilling both the blessings and the curses.

The faithfulness of God is paradoxical as it is bound up with His holiness and justice. By allowing the curses of the covenant to be realized, God is showing His loyalty to the promises made to Israel. This is God's faithful discipline, rooted in the covenant and pointing forward to eventual restoration.

Deuteronomy 28: Blessings and Curses in Lamentations

The connection between Deuteronomy 28, which outlines blessings for obedience and curses for disobedience, and Lamentations 3 is clear. The chapter in Lamentations records how Israel's faithlessness has resulted in the full realization of the curses that were outlined by Moses. These curses were intended to serve as results of Israel's unfaithfulness, and Lamentations 3 underscores how these consequences were not arbitrary but were part of the natural result of breaking the covenant.

Deuteronomy 28 presents a stark dichotomy: blessings for obedience and curses for disobedience. The blessings include prosperity, victory over enemies, and protection from harm, while the curses encompass defeat, disease, famine, exile, and social decay. Lamentations 3 reflects the latter. Suffering, desolation, and exile are the result of Israel's disobedience. Through these elements of suffering, Jeremiah points to God's faithfulness, acknowledging that God's justice in fulfilling the curses is an aspect of His faithful covenant-keeping.

Reward-Result Framework in Lamentations

The reward-result framework helps us interpret the relationship between blessings and curses in Lamentations 3. In this framework, God's rewards are the natural outcome of obedience, and His judgments are the natural result of disobedience. God's faithfulness to His word is demonstrated in both His promises of blessing and His warnings of judgment.

Deuteronomy Reference	Lamentations Reference	Specific Blessing/ Curse	Connection/ Explanation
Deuteronomy 28:52 (Destruction of city walls)	Lamentations 3:11	Destruction and vulnerability	The destruction of the city is a clear reflection of the failure of Jerusalem's defenses, as prophesied in the curses.

Deuteronomy Reference	Lamentations Reference	Specific Blessing/ Curse	Connection/ Explanation
Deuteronomy 28:53–57 (Famine, eating children during siege)	Lamentations 3:10–12	Severe famine, breakdown of society	Describes the horrors of famine and its extreme consequences, echoing the curses of eating one's own children in siege conditions.
Deuteronomy 28:63–64 (Scattering across nations)	Lamentations 3:22	Exile and dispersion	God's faithfulness despite the scattering of Israel reflects His covenant-keeping even in exile.
Deuteronomy 28:59–61 (Disease and pestilence)	Lamentations 3:4, 9	Disease and physical suffering	Lamentations 3 speaks to bodily suffering, echoing the pestilence curses in Deuteronomy.

Deuteronomy Reference	Lamentations Reference	Specific Blessing/ Curse	Connection/ Explanation
Deuteronomy 28:55 (Failure of safety and security)	Lamentations 3:9, 18	Insecurity and loss of hope	Lamentations speaks to the loss of stability and provision, directly relating to the curse of insecurity.
Deuteronomy 28:64 (Desperation, permanent desolation)	Lamentations 3:22–23	Permanent exile and desolation	While God is faithful, Lamentations highlights the permanent nature of exile due to disobedience, fulfilling God's curses.

God's Justice and Faithfulness

Through Lamentations 3, we see that God's justice does not negate His faithfulness. God is faithful in judgment, and the fulfillment of the curses is part of His faithfulness to uphold His covenant. The curses are not the end but rather the beginning of the path toward restoration. Even in the darkest moments when the consequences of sin are painfully evident, God remains faithful to His word and promises.

This paradox of God's faithfulness in judgment teaches an important lesson about the holiness of God and the seriousness of sin. The fulfillment of curses is not a departure from God's nature but rather a demonstration of His unwavering commitment to His covenant. Thus, even in the midst of suffering, the faithful can have hope in God's promises for restoration.

Conclusion: God's Faithfulness and Restoration

The book of Lamentations may seem to speak primarily of judgment and suffering, but its core message is one of hope in God's faithfulness. In Lamentations 3, the faithfulness of God is proclaimed even as Israel endures the results of her sin. This is not a contradiction but a reflection of God's unchanging nature. He fulfills both His promises of blessing and His warnings of judgment. Yet even in judgment there is hope for restoration, for God is faithful to bring His people back.

As we reflect on Lamentations 3, we are reminded that God's faithfulness is not only seen in His blessings but also in His judgment. Through the reward-result framework, we understand that the blessings and curses in Deuteronomy 28 are not arbitrary but are a direct result of obedience and disobedience. God's faithfulness in judgment is a call to repentance but also a promise of restoration because His covenant remains steadfast.

Study Guide for Chapter 10

The Book of Lamentations: God's Faithfulness Amidst Judgment

Summary:
Interprets Jerusalem's fall through covenant categories; God remains faithful in judgment.

Discussion Questions:

1. How does Lamentations reflect Deuteronomy 28?

2. What does the book reveal about God's character in suffering?

3. How can grief coexist with hope?

Application:

Write a prayer of lament patterned after Lamentations.

Scripture Reflection: Lamentations 3:22–23

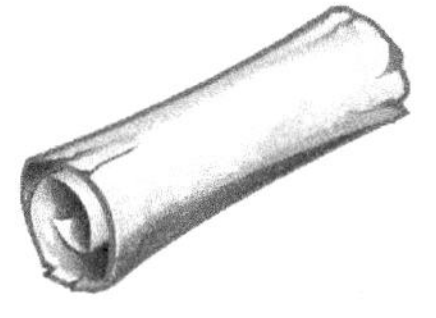

Chapter 11:

THE REVIVAL UNDER EZRA AND NEHEMIAH: RETURNING TO THE DECALOGUE

The books of Ezra and Nehemiah document one of the most significant revivals in Israel's history: the return of the Jewish exiles from Babylon and the reestablishment of worship in Jerusalem. The key element of this revival was the renewed commitment to God's law, particularly the Decalogue. This chapter focuses on the role of the law in the revival led by Ezra and Nehemiah, and how it demonstrates a return to the foundational moral law as a guide for Israel's spiritual and communal life.

The revival in Ezra and Nehemiah is not just about physical rebuilding, although the rebuilding of the Temple and the walls of Jerusalem were important symbols of the restoration of God's covenant presence. More profoundly, this revival was about the restoration of the people's relationship with God through a renewed understanding of the law, particularly the Ten Commandments, which served as the moral foundation for the life of God's people.

Ezra and the Restoration of the Law

Ezra, a priest and scribe, plays a central role in the revival by leading the people in the study and application of the law. In Ezra 7:10, Ezra "devoted himself to the study and observance of the law of the Lord, and to teaching its decrees and laws in Israel." This reflects Ezra's dual role as both teacher and model for the people. His primary task was to lead the people in returning to a right understanding of God's Word, and specifically the law.

When Ezra arrived in Jerusalem, the people were spiritually disoriented. Although they had returned from exile and rebuilt the Temple, they were living in a state of compromise with the surrounding cultures. Ezra's mission was to restore the spiritual health of the nation by calling the people back to their covenant obligations as expressed in the law of God.

In Ezra 9–10, we see Ezra's response to the people's intermarriage with foreign nations and their neglect of the covenant. He prays a heartfelt prayer of confession (Ezra 9:6–15), acknowledging his own and Israel's sins and the failure to live according to God's moral law. The people respond by repenting and reaffirming their commitment to God's law, specifically in areas of separation from idolatry and a renewed commitment to obey the moral law of God. This highlights how the Ten Commandments were seen as the foundational moral principles for guiding the nation's spiritual and societal renewal.

Nehemiah and the Renewal of the Covenant

While Ezra focused on the teaching of the law, Nehemiah's role was more focused on practical leadership, particularly in the rebuilding of the city walls and the restoration of a secure, functioning community. However, his efforts were deeply tied to the spiritual renewal happening under Ezra's leadership.

In Nehemiah 8–9, a profound spiritual awakening takes place. The people gather to hear Ezra read from the Book of the law, and they weep upon hearing it, recognizing how far they had fallen from God's standards. This emotional response signifies a deep sense of conviction and regret over their disobedience to God's Word.

In Nehemiah 9:1–3, the people gather for a public confession of sins and a renewal of the covenant. As part of the process, they commit themselves to follow God's commands, particularly the moral principles expressed in the Decalogue. This renewal of the covenant highlights the importance of the law as the guiding principle for the nation's life, even as they faced challenges and rebuilding after exile.

The public reading of the law (Neh. 8:2–8) is particularly significant because it reveals how the Decalogue was not simply a list of commands but a living guide for the people's relationship with God and their ethical behavior toward one another. The moral law served as the moral compass for the nation and was seen as essential to their covenant relationship with God.

The Role of the Decalogue in the Revival

The revival under Ezra and Nehemiah demonstrates that the Decalogue was central to the people's spiritual renewal. The Ten Commandments provided the moral framework that undergirded the community's obedience to God's will. The people understood that God's commands were not just rules to follow but were principles that shaped the character of the community and their relationship with God.

Through the teachings of Ezra and Nehemiah, we see a return to the centrality of the law in the life of God's people. The Decalogue, in particular, served as the standard for both individual morality and communal justice. The revival marked a return to covenant faithfulness, with the law as the defining factor in how Israel was to live as God's people.

The moral principles laid out in the Ten Commandments served as a guide for their ethics, from honoring parents to loving neighbors, and from avoiding falsehood to resting on the Sabbath. These commandments, along with the other applications of the law found in the Book of the Covenant (Exod. 19–24), set the tone for a community life that was both spiritually vibrant and ethically grounded.

Conclusion: A Model for Today

The revival under Ezra and Nehemiah serves as a powerful model for how God's law should be central to the life of the believer and the community. The Decalogue was not merely an historical artifact but principles of eternal relevance for right living before God. Just as the return to the law marked Israel's spiritual renewal, so too should the study and application of God's law serve as a foundation for the spiritual health of the Church today.

In our contemporary context, the law of God, as seen in the Ten Commandments, remains a moral guide that shapes our understanding of God's will for our lives. like the Israelites in the time of Ezra and Nehemiah, we are called to renew our commitment to live according to God's moral standards, to honor Him in our relationships, and to pursue lives that reflect His holiness.

Study Guide for Chapter 11

The Revival Under Ezra and Nehemiah: Returning to the Decalogue

---

Summary:
Revival begins with rediscovering and recommitting to the Law.

Discussion Questions:

1. Why is Scripture central to spiritual renewal?

2. What practices in Ezra–Nehemiah model healthy communal discipleship?

3. How can modern churches emulate this revival pattern?

Application:

Commit to a daily Scripture rhythm for one week.

Scripture Reflection: Nehemiah 8

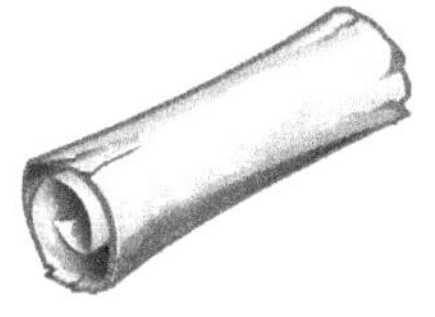

Chapter 12: THE SERMON ON THE MOUNT: JESUS RESTORES THE TRUE MEANING OF THE LAW

The Sermon on the Mount (Matt. 5–7) is one of the most significant teachings of Jesus in the New Testament where He presents not just an ethical framework but a restoration of the true meaning of the law. For many, the Sermon on the Mount has been seen as a reinterpretation or even an overturning of the Old Testament law. However, this view is a misunderstanding of Jesus's intent. Rather than reinterpreting the law, Jesus is restoring its original meaning that had been distorted over time by misinterpretations and legalism, particularly by the Pharisees and teachers of the law.

Jesus's Teachings on the Law

In the Beatitudes, Jesus presents a transformative journey that aligns with the Being, Knowing, Doing framework, beginning with the internal transformation of the individual's Being. Jesus starts with poverty of spirit where the believer recognizes their spiritual bankruptcy, acknowledging that they have nothing to offer before God. This recognition leads to mourning, a grieving over their spiritual condition. Out of this mourning comes meekness, a humbling and submission of the self to God's will, which results in power under control. This meekness reflects the Being of the believer as they are shaped into a person who is no longer self-reliant but fully reliant on God.

The transformation continues with a hunger and thirst for righteousness, a longing to align our life with God's will and His holiness. As the believer's Being is reshaped, this transformation overflows into action, or doing. The believer, now empowered by this inner change, becomes merciful, pure in heart, and a peacemaker, reflecting the fruits of the Spirit. Yet as this new identity takes shape, the believer may face persecution because the world does not easily accept the radically different lifestyle that God's Kingdom demands. Thus, Jesus outlines the process where Being leads to Knowing (a deep recognition of your new identity in Christ), which ultimately shapes doing (a life lived in mercy, purity, and peace). This progression from poverty of spirit to persecution is the journey of spiritual growth, laying the foundation for living the law not just outwardly but from the heart.

In the Sermon on the Mount, Jesus makes it clear that His interpretation of the law is not a new set of rules or a contradiction to what came before but rather a clarification of what the law was always meant to convey. He highlights the deeper moral and spiritual intent behind the commandments, demonstrating that true righteousness is not just about external conformity but about an inner transformation of the heart.

The Sermon on the Mount is full of teachings that build upon the Old Testament commandments, showing that they were not meant to be legalistic rules but were moral principles that pointed to the need for a transformed life.

The First Commandment ("you shall have no other gods before me") is explained in Matthew 6:19–24 where Jesus speaks about the dangers of materialism and warns against treasuring earthly things that compete with God for our affections. Jesus makes clear that a divided heart will lead to spiritual ruin and that loving God alone requires the whole heart.

The Second Commandment (no idols) is explained in Matthew 6:24 where Jesus says, "No one can serve two masters." This teaching connects the idea of idolatry with the issue of loyalty and devotion. The commandment against idolatry is not only about avoiding physical idols but also about avoiding anything that competes with God for our allegiance.

The Third Commandment (do not misuse God's name) is addressed in Matthew 6:9 where Jesus instructs His disciples to pray to the Father, "Hallowed be your name." This emphasizes that God's name is to be revered and kept holy, reinforcing that respect for God's holiness is integral to the believer's relationship with Him.

The Fourth Commandment (remember the Sabbath day and keep it holy) is expounded in Matthew 6:25–34 where Jesus calls His followers to trust in God for their needs, showing that rest and Sabbath are rooted in trusting God's provision and relying on His care, not just ritual observance.

Jesus's Teaching on the Ten Commandments in the Sermon on the Mount

In Matthew 5:17–48, Jesus specifically addresses the moral law as presented in the Ten Commandments (Exod. 20) and shows how its principles should be understood and applied in the lives of His followers. Jesus does not diminish the commandments but emphasizes their deep spiritual significance. He applies each of the fifth through tenth commandments, bringing them to a fuller understanding and showing that their true meaning extends beyond outward obedience to an internal transformation of the heart.

The Fifth Commandment: Honor Your Father and Your Mother

In Matthew 5:17–20, Jesus does not directly quote this commandment but emphasizes its broader application to honor and respect in the community. Jesus's broader treatment of honoring others connects this command to a heart attitude that respects God's authority and order, starting with your parents. This speaks to the broader theme of honoring God's authority in all relationships.

The Sixth Commandment: Do Not Murder

In Matthew 5:21–26, Jesus directly addresses the sixth commandment, stating that it's not just the act of murder that violates God's will but also anger and hatred toward others. He teaches that even harboring anger in the heart can lead to spiritual harm, showing that the root of murder is found in sinful emotions and attitudes. True righteousness, according to Jesus, involves reconciliation and peace-making with others, not just avoiding violence.

The Seventh Commandment: Do Not Commit Adultery

In Matthew 5:27–32, Jesus directly addresses the seventh commandment, extending its meaning to include lustful thoughts. Jesus teaches that adultery is not limited to physical actions but includes intentions of the heart. Purity of heart and faithfulness in marriage are central to fulfilling this commandment, and Jesus calls His followers to radically avoid situations that may lead to temptation.

The Ninth Commandment: Do Not Bear False Witness

In Matthew 5:33–37, Jesus refers to the ninth commandment concerning falsehood and lying. He teaches that integrity in speech is of utmost importance, saying that your word should be trusted without the need for oaths. This commandment extends beyond legal contexts to every aspect of life, urging believers to speak truthfully and live with integrity in all their relationships. Truth-telling is seen as a reflection of God's faithfulness and justice.

The Eighth Commandment: Do Not Steal

In Matthew 5:38–42, Jesus addresses the eighth commandment by teaching about non-retaliation and generosity. While the commandment forbids theft, Jesus explains that it includes a life marked by selflessness and generosity. The teaching challenges believers to act counterculturally by offering more than what is required, being gracious even when wronged. Jesus emphasizes that true righteousness involves a life of sacrificial giving and non-retaliation.

The Tenth Commandment: Do Not Covet

In Matthew 5:43–48, Jesus speaks to the tenth commandment by teaching about love for enemies and loving our neighbors as ourselves. He explains that covetousness is not merely about material possessions but also about selfishness and jealousy toward others. True fulfillment of the tenth commandment comes through a heart that is free from envy, seeks the flourishing of others, and loves without conditions. Jesus calls His followers to a higher standard, one that reflects the unconditional love of God.

Jesus and the Reward-Result Framework in Matthew 6

In Matthew 6, Jesus contrasts two different frameworks for understanding rewards: the "wage" mentality of the Pharisees and the "result" mentality he encourages his followers to adopt. In his examples of giving, praying, and fasting, Jesus challenges the prevalent pharisaical attitude of performing these actions in public to gain a visible reward (*misthon*)—essentially a "wage" earned through outward actions. However, Jesus calls His disciples to a different way: to practice these disciplines in secret, not for a wage but for a result (*apodidomai*). This subtle yet significant shift emphasizes that true reward comes not from human recognition or compensation but from the outcome of living according to God's will. In the context of seeking the Kingdom of God, as Jesus concludes in Matthew 6:33, this "result" is not earned or demanded but flows naturally from a life devoted to God. The shift from seeking a "wage" to desiring a "result" aligns with Jesus's overall teaching about God's Kingdom, a kingdom where the pursuit of holiness and obedience leads to blessings, not as payment but as natural outcomes of living in alignment with God's purposes.

The Heart of the Law: Internal Transformation

One of the key themes of the Sermon on the Mount is that true righteousness is not about external compliance to a set of rules but about a radical transformation of the heart. Jesus does not say that the law is wrong or unnecessary; rather, He calls

His followers to the higher standard, one that begins with a renewed heart and mind.

For example, in Matthew 5:21–22, Jesus addresses the sixth commandment, "You shall not murder," and explains its breadth, saying that anger toward a brother or sister is just as grievous as murder. He shows that the root of sin lies in the heart, and the law's true purpose is to transform people from the inside out.

Similarly, in Matthew 5:27–28, Jesus addresses the seventh commandment, "You shall not commit adultery." He says that even lusting after someone in the heart is committing adultery in the mind. Here, Jesus highlights the importance of purity of heart and thought, not just actions.

In Matthew 5:33–37, Jesus addresses the ninth commandment, "You shall not give false testimony." He teaches that instead of swearing oaths to prove honesty, believers should simply let their yes be yes and their no be no. This emphasis on truthfulness and integrity reflects the deeper moral purpose of the law, which calls for honesty at all levels of life, not just in legal or formal situations.

Conclusion: Jesus and the Fulfillment of the Law

In the Sermon on the Mount, Jesus reveals that the law is not just about external adherence to rules but about a deep transformation of the heart. He fulfills the law by revealing its true purpose—not to merely be obeyed outwardly but to guide His followers toward godly living that reflects the character of God.

Jesus shows that true righteousness comes from a heart transformed by grace, not from simply following rules.

Jesus's interpretation of the law is not a rejection of the Old Testament but a restoration of its original intent. By emphasizing the heart behind the commandments, Jesus calls His followers to live out the moral law in a way that demonstrates God's love, justice, and mercy in a broken world. In this way, the Sermon on the Mount becomes the fullest revelation of how the moral law is to be applied in the Kingdom of God where the heart and the actions are aligned with God's will.

Study Guide for Chapter 12

The Sermon on the Mount:
Jesus Restores the True Meaning of the Law

Summary:
Jesus restores the Law's original heart-intent and clarifies true righteousness.

Discussion Questions:

1. How does Jesus explain the deeper meaning of each commandment?

2. What is the difference between misthon and apodidomai?

3. Why does Jesus focus on internal transformation?

Application:

Reflect on one internal attitude needing transformation.

Scripture Reflection: Matthew 5–7

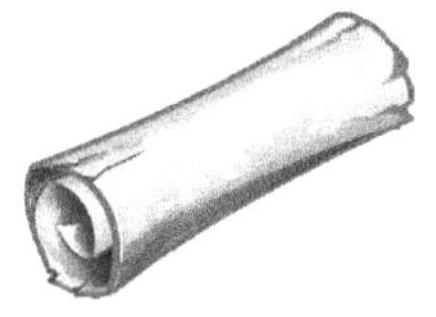

Chapter 13: ROMANS AND THE BEING, KNOWING, DOING FRAMEWORK

The book of Romans stands as one of the most comprehensive and profound writings of the Apostle Paul on the gospel and its application to the lives of believers. It serves as a foundational epistle for understanding the gospel's scope, from the justification of sinners by faith to the sanctification of believers through the Holy Spirit. One of the most insightful ways to organize the themes of Romans is through the Being, Knowing, Doing framework. This framework, which we have explored earlier, provides a structured way to understand how the gospel is applied to the believer's life—first in Being, who we are in Christ; then in Knowing, understanding the implications of our new identity in Christ; and finally in Doing, living out this identity in practical ways.

Romans 1–4: Being - Justification by Faith

The first section of Romans (chapters 1–4) deals primarily with the Being of the believer. This section answers the foundational question by what power can I keep God's law?. Paul begins by demonstrating the universal sinfulness of humanity and the inability of the law to justify anyone before God. In these chapters, the righteousness of God is revealed through faith, and justification is received by faith, not by works of the law.

Paul uses Abraham as an example of justification by faith in Romans 4, demonstrating that even Abraham was declared righteous before God, not because of his works but because of his faith in God's promises (Rom. 4:3). This establishes the key point of Romans 1–4: Justification is a gift of grace, received through faith in Jesus Christ and not by human effort.

The Greek term *pistis* (faith) is used prominently in this section. In fact, the word appears twenty-five times in Romans 1–4, emphasizing that faith is the central mechanism by which believers are made right with God. Paul contrasts this faith with human works and shows that no one can be justified by keeping the law. The use of *pistis* in these chapters underscores the importance of trusting in God's provision through Christ for righteousness rather than relying on human effort.

Romans 5-8: Knowing - Implications of the New Identity in Christ

Having established the believer's new identity in Christ through justification by faith, Paul moves to the Knowing aspect in chapters 5–8. Here, Paul elaborates on the implications of this new identity, explaining the transformative power of grace and the Holy Spirit. In Romans 5, Paul emphasizes that through faith in Christ, believers now have peace with God (Rom. 5:1), are reconciled to God, and can rejoice in the hope of the glory of God. These truths establish the foundation for understanding how believers are to live out their new identity.

Romans 6:3–9 shows that believers have been united with Christ in His death and resurrection. Through baptism, believers are called to live in newness of life, and sin no longer has dominion over them. This is the Knowing aspect where believers are to know and understand their new position in Christ—dead to sin but alive to God.

Romans 6:11 provides a crucial passage where Paul instructs believers to consider (Greek: *logizomai*) themselves dead to sin and alive to God. This is a critical part of the Knowing framework. Paul is urging believers to know and reckon their new identity in Christ, internalizing the reality that they are free from the power of sin.

In Romans 7, Paul addresses the tension between the believer's new identity and the ongoing struggle with sin. He illustrates the conflict between the flesh and the Spirit, and in Romans 8, he declares that the Holy Spirit empowers believers to live according to God's will. The Spirit enables them to live victorious lives where sin is no longer their master (Rom. 8:13).

One of the key Greek terms used in this section is *zoe* (life). Whereas *pistis* (faith) is central in Romans 1–4, *zoe* (life) is used extensively in chapters 5–8. The word *zoe* appears twenty-five times in this section, emphasizing the new life believers have in Christ. In Romans 6:4, Paul speaks of walking in newness of life, and in Romans 8:6, he explains that the mind set on the Spirit is life and peace. The word *zoe* here speaks of the quality of life that believers experience as a result of their union with Christ through the Holy Spirit.

Romans 6: The Being, Knowing, Doing Framework

Romans 6 provides a clear demonstration of the Being, Knowing, Doing framework. In this chapter, Paul outlines a threefold process for the believer.

Know (Being)

In Romans 6:3, Paul says, "Don't you know that all of us who were baptized into Christ Jesus were baptized into His death?" The believer's identity is now in Christ, and this new identity is defined by Christ's death and resurrection.

In Romans 6:9, Paul emphasizes that Christ's resurrection is the guarantee of the believer's new life and freedom from the power of sin.

Consider (Knowing)

Romans 6:11 states, "Count yourselves dead to sin but alive to God in Christ." This is the Knowing aspect. Believers must consciously reckon themselves to be dead to sin and alive to God. This inner realization is key to the process of transformation.

Present (Doing)

In Romans 6:13, Paul writes, "Do not offer any part of yourself to sin as an instrument of wickedness, but rather offer yourselves to God as those who have been brought from death to life." Here, Paul calls believers to actively present their lives to God in service, reflecting the Doing aspect of the framework. This involves action—choosing righteousness over sin and living in a way that honors God.

Thus, Romans 6 encapsulates the Being, Knowing, Doing framework as it relates to the believer's new life in Christ. Being is the foundation of the believer's new identity. Knowing involves recognizing and internalizing this new identity. And Doing refers to the practical outworking of that identity in daily life.

Thus, Paul answers his question: by what power can I keep God's law? His answer is that it is the power inherent in our changed being.

The Three Uses of the Law: Convict, Bridle, and Guide (a Fourth Framework)

As we examine the application of the law in the believer's life, it is important to consider the three uses of the law, a framework that Paul recognizes throughout Romans. These three uses of the law can be summarized as convict, bridle, and guide.

Convict: The first use of the law is its ability to convict people of sin. In Romans 3:19–20, Paul explains that the law has the role of making people aware of their sinfulness. This is a necessary prerequisite to a change in Being. It reveals the depth of humanity's rebellion against God and convicts people of their need for a Savior. The law functions as a mirror that exposes our sin but does not have the power to save.

Bridle: The second use of the law is to restrain evil in society. In Romans 13:1–7, Paul teaches that the law, including civil law, serves as a bridle. It helps maintain order and restrains evil by punishing wrongdoers. The law serves a societal function, ensuring that people do not live according to their sinful impulses but rather live in an orderly, peaceful manner.

Guide: The third use of the law is to serve as a guide for the believer's life. Once justified by faith, the believer is no longer under the curse of the law but is still called to live in accordance with God's moral standards. The moral law becomes a guide for how believers are to live, demonstrating what it means to love God and love others. In Romans 8:4, Paul explains that the righteous requirement of the law is fulfilled in believers who walk according to the Spirit. The law does not save, but it guides believers in how to live out their new identity in Christ.

For the believer, the law is primarily a guide, helping us live lives that reflect God's character. It points us to the moral will of God, teaching us how to love, honor, and serve Him and others. In Romans 7, Paul speaks of the law as holy, righteous, and good (Rom. 7:12), showing that it remains valuable to the believer as a means of living in the fullness of God's will.

Greek Terms: *Pistis* and *Zoe* in Romans

As mentioned before, one of the most striking features of Paul's structure in Romans is his use of the Greek terms *pistis* (faith) and *zoe* (life). These terms help highlight the central themes of justification and sanctification in the life of the believer.

The term *pistis* (faith) appears twenty-five times in Romans 1–4, underscoring the importance of faith in the process of justification. Faith is the means by which we receive God's righteousness, and it is through faith that the believer is declared righteous before God. However, in Romans 5–8, the focus shifts to the new life that believers experience in Christ, which is most clearly signified by the Greek term *zoe* (life).

In Romans 5–8, *zoe* appears twenty-five times, highlighting the new life believers now possess through the Holy Spirit. This section of Paul's letter emphasizes the transformation from death to life as believers are united with Christ in His resurrection, living new lives empowered by the Spirit.

Key Verses:

> *Romans 1:17:* "For in the gospel the righteousness of God is revealed—a righteousness that is by faith from first to last, just as it is written: 'The righteous will live by faith.'"

Romans 6:4: "We were therefore buried with him through baptism into death in order that, just as Christ was raised from the dead through the glory of the Father, we too may live a new life."

Romans 6:11: "In the same way, count yourselves dead to sin but alive to God in Christ Jesus."

Romans 8:6: "The mind governed by the flesh is death, but the mind governed by the Spirit is life and peace."

Conclusion: The Being, Knowing, Doing Framework in Romans

Romans presents the gospel as a transformative message that affects all aspects of the believer's life. Through the Being, Knowing, Doing framework, Paul outlines the full scope of the Christian life, from the identity we have in Christ to the understanding of that identity, to the practical outworking of this new life. The gospel is not only a message of justification but also one of transformation where believers are called to live in accordance with the will of God, empowered by the Holy Spirit, and reflected in their relationships with God and others.

Study Guide for Chapter 13

Romans and the Being, Knowing, Doing Framework

Summary:

Paul's structure—Being, Knowing, Doing—explains Spirit-enabled obedience and the uses of the Law.

Discussion Questions:

1. Why does obedience flow from identity?

2. What are the three uses of the Law?

3. How does Romans 6 connect knowing and doing?

Application:

Identify one truth about your identity that strengthens obedience.

Scripture Reflection: Romans 6

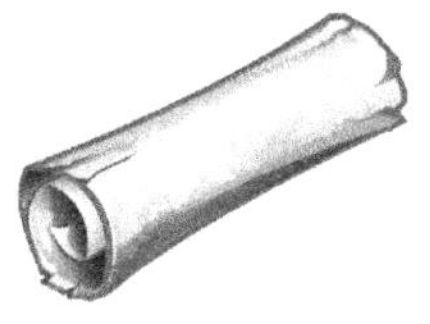

Chapter 14:

THE LAW IN THE BOOK OF JAMES: LIVING OUT THE LAW OF LIBERTY

I. Introduction: The Context of James's Teachings on the Law

James, the brother of Jesus, occupies a unique position in the New Testament canon. As both a leader of the Jerusalem church and a direct witness to the life and teachings of Jesus, James's understanding of the law is deeply informed by his familial relationship with the Savior. His epistle provides a practical application of the law, stressing that true obedience to God is not merely a matter of external rule-following but an expression of inner transformation and living faith. In his teachings, we see a continuity with Jesus's own perspective on the law, that it is a law of liberty, not of legalistic bondage, designed to guide the believer into holy living.

James's audience—Jewish believers dispersed throughout the Roman Empire (James 1:1)—were called to integrate their faith with daily living. James states that the law is not just a set of arbitrary rules but a means through which believers can reflect God's holiness and wisdom to the world. As we explore James's approach to the law, we'll see how it emphasizes moral and relational obligations, echoing the teachings of his brother Jesus.

II. James's Concept of the Law: The Law of Liberty

A. The Law as Perfect and Beneficial (James 1:25)

James introduces the law as the "perfect law that gives freedom" (James 1:25). Contrary to the then-common view of the Pharisees, the law is not a restrictive set of rules but a source of freedom. The term "perfect law" indicates that God's commandments are flawless, providing a clear path to righteousness. In the context of the New Covenant, this law is not burdensome but liberating because it guides believers in the way of holiness and flourishing. It helps believers live lives that are pleasing to God, fulfilling their ultimate purpose.

This theme mirrors Jesus's own view of the law. In Matthew 11:30, Jesus says, "For my yoke is easy, and my burden is light." The law, when rightly understood and applied, is not oppressive but rather a tool for flourishing and freedom. The law reveals what it means to live in alignment with God's will, offering freedom from sin and the consequences of disobedience.

B. The Law of Liberty: Freedom Through Obedience

James refers to the law as giving freedom in James 2:12: "Speak and act as those who are going to be judged by the law that gives freedom." For James, this is not a contradiction; obedience to the law is not a means of bondage but a pathway to freedom. Just as Jesus taught that the truth sets people free (John 8:32), James presents the law as a vehicle for spiritual freedom. It is the freedom to live as God intended—free from sin, free from condemnation, and free to reflect His character in the world.

The law of freedom is rooted in grace. Just as Israel's obedience to the law was a response to God's redemptive acts (Deut. 6:1–3), the Christian's obedience to the law is a response to the grace received through Christ. The law, then, is a guide for living the redeemed life, a life that reflects God's holiness and love.

III. James on the Relationship Between Faith and Works (James 2:14-26)

A. The Law and the Necessity of Works

James emphasizes that faith without works is dead (James 2:17), arguing that true faith is always accompanied by works. The law, in James's view, provides the framework for what constitutes good works. Believers are not saved by works but are called to demonstrate their faith through works of righteousness, in keeping with the law.

James's argument aligns with Jesus's teaching in the Sermon on the Mount where He explains that the "fruit" of a person's life reveals the condition of their heart (Matt. 7:16–20). For James, the law is not just a matter of outward compliance but an internal transformation that results in visible obedience. Fulfilling the royal law of love—"love your neighbor as yourself" (James 2:8)—becomes the hallmark of true faith and obedience.

B. Breaking the Law and Its Consequences

James also warns that if someone breaks one part of the law, they are guilty of breaking all of it (James 2:10). This highlights the seriousness of obedience to God's commandments. The law is unified, and even the smallest infraction carries weight because it reflects a heart that is not fully aligned with God's will. However, James also emphasizes mercy, showing that God's mercy triumphs over judgment (James 2:13), echoing Jesus's teachings on forgiveness and grace (Matt. 5:7).

IV. James and the Royal Law: "Love Your Neighbor as Yourself"

A. Central Role of the Royal Law in James

James repeatedly refers to the "royal law" (James 2:8), which is found in Leviticus 19:18 and was central to Jesus's teachings. The command to "love your neighbor as yourself" is the summation of the law's ethical demands. For James, this law encapsulates the essence of godly living. Obedience to this law involves treating others with justice, fairness, and mercy, and it forms the foundation of Christian ethics.

Jesus reinforced this law in Matthew 22:39, and James echoes this when he condemns favoritism in the church (James 2:1–7). Partiality contradicts the law of love and undermines the unity of the body of Christ.

B. The Law and Partiality

James condemns partiality, especially in the context of rich and poor (James 2:1–7). For James, treating people differently based on their social status is a violation of the royal law. True obedience to God's law involves seeing all people as equal in dignity and worth, regardless of their external circumstances.

This principle resonates with Jesus's ministry where He showed love and compassion to the marginalized, the poor, and the outcast. By following the royal law, Christians reflect God's impartiality and His love for all people.

C. The Call to Mercy

James 2:13 emphasizes that "mercy triumphs over judgment." For James, mercy is not just an emotional response but an active obedience to God's command to love and serve others. This mercy reflects the heart of the law and is an essential aspect of Christian living. Jesus also taught that mercy was central to God's character and that His followers should imitate this mercy in their relationships with others (Matt. 5:7).

V. James and the Use of the Law in the New Covenant

A. The Law of the Spirit and the Believer's Relationship to It

James views the law through the lens of the New Covenant where the Holy Spirit empowers believers to live out God's commandments. While the law is still relevant, and was never, as the Pharisees implied, about mere external obedience but about an internal transformation brought about by the Spirit. Believers are called to obey, not out of legalistic obligation but as a response to the work of Christ within them.

B. Jesus as the Fulfillment of the Law

Jesus's life and teachings fulfill the law, not by abolishing it but by fulfilling its true intent. As James was closely connected to Jesus, his teachings reflect the same understanding of the law as Jesus's—the law is not a set of arbitrary rules but a reflection of God's will and character. In Christ, believers find the ultimate fulfillment of the law's demands.

VI. Conclusion: James's Take on the Law and the Christian Life

James presents the law as a guide for living out the Christian faith. For James, the law is not merely a set of rules but a way of life that reflects God's wisdom, love, and justice. The law of liberty calls believers to live in freedom, demonstrating their faith through works of righteousness and love. James's emphasis on the law aligns with Jesus's teachings. Both call for a holistic approach to obedience, one that integrates heart, mind, and action. By living out the royal law of love and mercy, believers fulfill their calling to be a light to the world, reflecting the character of God in all aspects of life.

Study Guide for Chapter 14

The Law in the Book of James: Living Out the Law of Liberty

Summary:

The Law of Liberty produces action—faith works itself out in obedience.

Discussion Questions:

1. How does James define the Law of Liberty?

2. Why does faith require works?

3. What does James teach about partiality?

Application:

Practice an act of mercy this week.

Scripture Reflection: James 1:25

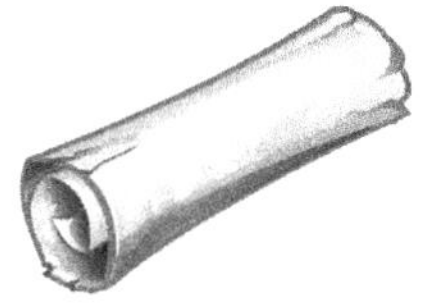

Chapter 15:

THE LAW AND THE NEW COVENANT: THE BELIEVER'S RESPONSIBILITY TO THE LAW

The question of how the law relates to the New Covenant is central to understanding the role of the believer in the modern era. The New Covenant ("new" indicating completed, not different) established through the life, death, and resurrection of Jesus Christ radically changes the believer's relationship to the law. However, it is essential to understand the Covenant of Grace framework, which shapes our understanding of the law and its application throughout redemptive history.

The Covenant of Grace is the overarching framework that governs the relationship between God and His people throughout redemptive history. It begins with God's promise to Adam and Eve after the fall, that the Seed of the woman would crush the serpent's head (Gen. 3:15). This promise points to the coming of Christ and is the foundation of the Covenant of Grace that will unfold throughout the Scriptures.

In Genesis 6–9, God establishes the covenant with Noah, promising never to destroy the earth with a flood again and reaffirming the grace that will be available through the coming Seed. The covenant with Abraham (Gen. 12–50) further develops the promise of grace as God chooses Abraham and his descendants to be a blessing to all nations.

The covenant with Moses (Exodus–Deuteronomy) is often considered the Old Covenant but should be understood as part of the unfolding Covenant of Grace. While the covenant with Adam was based on perfect obedience (Covenant of Works), the Mosaic Covenant is given in the context of grace to a people already delivered by God from slavery in Egypt. As such, the law given to Israel is never a means of earning salvation but rather a gracious guide for living in the presence of the Holy God.

The Law Given Within the Covenant of Grace

In this light, the law does not negate God's grace, nor does it offer a new condition for salvation. Instead, it is given as part of the Covenant of Grace and serves to show God's people how to live out their relationship with Him. It is a guide to reflect His character and bring about the flourishing of His people.

The Decalogue, or Ten Commandments, forms the heart of the moral law that governs the believer's life. Jesus did not come to abolish this law but to fulfill it. His interpretation of the law was not in contrast to the Ten Commandments but to the misunderstanding and misapplication of the law by the Pharisees. The Pharisees interpreted the Ten Commandments in a legalistic way, seeing them as a means to earn God's favor rather than understanding them as gracious guidelines given to a redeemed people.

The Pharisaic Misinterpretation of the Law

One of the primary reasons for the confusion between the Covenant of Works and the Covenant of Grace is the Pharisees' misinterpretation of the Decalogue. The Pharisees viewed the law as a means to earn salvation by external obedience, much like the Covenant of Works made with Adam. This view reduced the law to a set of legal requirements that, if followed meticulously, would grant the person acceptance before God.

However, Jesus's ministry constantly confronted this misinterpretation. In His teachings, particularly in the Sermon on the Mount, Jesus clarifies that the Ten Commandments were not merely external rules to follow but principles that reflect God's character and require a heart-level transformation. Jesus's criticisms of the Pharisees were not criticisms of the law itself but of how the Pharisees distorted it.

The Sermon on the Mount: Jesus's Contrast with the Pharisaic Interpretation

The Sermon on the Mount provides a powerful contrast between Jesus's true interpretation of the law and the pharisaic interpretation. In each instance where Jesus refers to one of the Ten Commandments, He begins by saying, "You have heard that it was said . . . but I say to you." This format highlights the difference between the pharisaic understanding of the law and Jesus's true intent.

In Matthew 5:21–22, Jesus addresses the sixth commandment ("do not murder"), but He explains its meaning by connecting it to anger and insulting others. He says, "Anyone who is angry with a brother or sister will be subject to judgment" (v. 22). Jesus shows that the commandment is not just about outward violence but about the heart's intent, demonstrating that the law was never only about external obedience.

In Matthew 5:27–28 on the seventh commandment ("do not commit adultery"), Jesus teaches that lustful thoughts are just as sinful as physical adultery. Again, Jesus highlights that the law addresses not just external actions but the condition of the heart, emphasizing the importance of inner purity.

In Matthew 5:33–37, Jesus addresses the ninth commandment ("do not bear false witness") by showing that speaking the truth is not just about avoiding falsehood but about being truthful in all things. He criticizes the pharisaic practice of swearing oaths to make their words more credible, teaching that the believer should be known for their integrity.

In each of these instances, Jesus interprets the Ten Commandments by showing that their true intent was always about the heart. The Pharisees had turned the law into a legalistic checklist, but Jesus calls His followers to a deeper, internal transformation that reflects God's holiness.

The Believer's Responsibility to the Law in the New Covenant

The New (completed) Covenant, established in Jesus Christ, transforms the believer's relationship to the law. The law is not abolished but fulfilled in Christ. The believer is not under the curse of the law since Christ has borne the penalty for sin, but the moral law continues to be relevant as a guide for living a life that reflects God's holiness.

In Romans 13:8–10, Paul affirms the relevance of the moral law in the New Covenant by stating that all the commandments can be summed up in the command to love your neighbor as yourself. Love is the fulfillment of the law because it reflects the character of God.

In Romans 8:4, Paul explains that through the Holy Spirit, the believer is empowered to live out the righteous requirements of the law. The Spirit enables the believer to obey God's commands, not through external effort but as a response to grace.

The New Covenant frees believers from the curse of the law but calls them to obedience out of love for God. The law, viewed this way, is no longer a burden to earn salvation but a guide that leads believers in living out their new identity in Christ.

The Law as a Guide to the Transformed Life

As believers, we are not under the legalistic demands of the law, but we are called to live out its moral principles in the power of the Holy Spirit. The Ten Commandments serve as a guide for how we are to love God and love others. Jesus's teachings in the Sermon on the Mount reveal that true obedience to the law comes from a transformed heart, and the believer is empowered to live in this way by the Spirit.

The law as a guide for the believer in the New Covenant is not about external conformity but about an internal change that flows from the heart. As we live by the Spirit, we are enabled to fulfill the righteous requirements of the law, reflecting the character of God and advancing His Kingdom in the world.

Conclusion: The Believer's Relationship to the Law in the New Covenant

In conclusion, the New Covenant reorients the believer's relationship to the law. The Covenant of Grace frames the believer's relationship to the law as it is not based on human effort but on God's gracious provision through Christ. The moral law is still relevant for the believer, but its fulfillment is now empowered by the Spirit, and its purpose is not to earn salvation but to guide the believer in obedient love. The Sermon on the Mount provides the key to understanding the true intent of the law, which was never about legalistic observance but about living according to the heart of God's commands.

Study Guide for Chapter 15

The Law and the New Covenant:
The Believer's Responsibility to the Law

Summary:

Jesus corrects Pharisaic misuse of the Law and restores its purpose as a guide for redeemed living.

Discussion Questions:

1. What misunderstanding did the Pharisees have about the Law?

2. How does Jesus restore the Law's intent?

3. Why is the Law still relevant in the New Covenant?

Application:

Surrender one area of legalism or license to Christ.

Scripture Reflection: Jeremiah 31:31–34

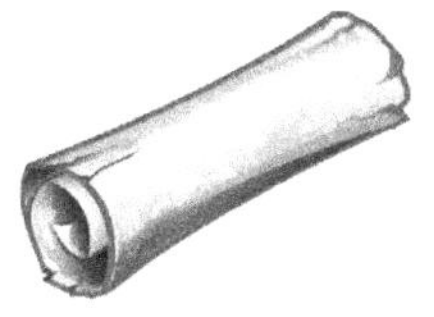

Chapter 16:

PRACTICAL APPLICATION FOR TODAY: UNDERSTANDING THE ROLE OF THE LAW IN THE BELIEVER'S LIFE

As we have explored in this book, the law of God remains a central theme in the life of the believer. The moral law, as expressed in the Ten Commandments, continues to guide and shape the believer's life, even under the New Covenant. However, this question remains: What is the practical role of the law in the believer's life today? How do we as believers in Christ understand and apply the moral principles of the law in a way that reflects our new identity in Christ and the grace given to us through the gospel?

In this chapter, we will explore the practical applications of the law for today, examining how the moral law still speaks to the believer's daily life. We will see how the law is not a burden or a means to earn God's favor but rather a guide that leads to spiritual maturity, a reflection of God's character, and a life of obedience to Him. This chapter will discuss how the law informs the believer's ethical choices, relationships, and conduct in the world, with an emphasis on how the Holy Spirit empowers believers to live in alignment with God's will.

The Law as a Guide for Ethical Living

The moral law given in the Ten Commandments serves as a guide for ethical living in the believer's daily life. While we are not under the curse of the law, the Ten Commandments continue to reflect God's character and moral standards. As believers, we are called to live lives that honor God and reflect His holiness in all areas of life.

One of the primary ways the law functions as a guide is in its ability to point believers to right conduct—how we should live in relationship to God and to others. Jesus summarizes the moral law in two commandments: "Love the Lord your God with all your heart, soul, and mind" (first four commandments) and "love your neighbor as yourself" (last six commandments). These two commandments provide a framework for understanding how the Ten Commandments should be applied today. As we live out these two principles, we are fulfilling the law by living lives of obedience and love.

For example, the first commandment, "You shall have no other gods before me" (Exod. 20:3), reminds believers of the centrality of God in their lives. In practical terms, this commandment calls us to examine our priorities and affections. Are we placing God above all other things, or are there idols in our lives that compete for our affections? This principle not only applies to material objects but can also refer to things such as relationships, ambitions, or even success, which can become idols if they take precedence over God's place in our lives.

Similarly, the sixth commandment, "You shall not murder" (Exod. 20:13), is not just about physical murder but about a heart of compassion toward others. In the Sermon on the Mount, Jesus expands this commandment to include anger and insulting words, showing that God cares deeply about how we treat others and that hatred and malice in the heart are just as serious as physical violence.

The Law as a Reflection of God's Character

One of the most important aspects of the law is that it reflects God's character. The Ten Commandments are not arbitrary rules but moral principles that stem from God's holiness, righteousness, and justice. As such, they reveal what it means to live according to God's will and in relationship with Him.

The law calls believers to imitate God's holiness, to reflect His justice and mercy, and to live out the character traits that He embodies. For example, the tenth commandment, "You shall not covet" (Exod. 20:17), reveals God's concern for the contentment of His people. The believer who obeys this commandment is expressing trust in God's provision and reflecting God's generosity rather than living in jealousy or envy. This principle speaks to the believer's attitude toward material possessions and the desire for contentment in all things.

In this way, the law serves as a mirror for the believer, revealing how we measure up to God's moral standards and showing us areas where we need to grow. The moral law functions as a guide to help believers live in a way that honors God's holiness and expresses love for others.

The Role of the Holy Spirit in Living Out the Law

It is important to recognize that the law is not something we can obey in our own strength. The Holy Spirit, who dwells in the believer, empowers us to live out the righteous requirements of the law. The Holy Spirit transforms the hearts of believers, enabling them to live according to God's will and reflect His character. "In order that the righteous requirement of the law might be fully met in us, who do not live according to the flesh but according to the Spirit" (Rom. 8:4). "So I say, walk by the Spirit, and you will not gratify the desires of the flesh" (Gal. 5:16).

The Holy Spirit Is the one who enables believers to live a life that reflects the character of Christ. As believers, we are not under the condemnation of the law, but we are still called to live out its principles. The Spirit empowers us to obey God's commands, not out of duty or fear but out of gratitude and love for the grace we have received. The fruit of the Spirit (Gal. 5:22–23) is the natural outgrowth of this transformation as the believer's life becomes marked by love, joy, peace, patience, kindness, and all the other virtues that reflect God's character.

The Law and the Believer's Ethical Decisions

The law also plays a significant role in the ethical decisions believers face in everyday life. The moral law helps the believer discern what is right and wrong in situations where there is no explicit biblical command. In these cases, the law serves as a guide to living in a way that honors God and reflects His will.

For instance, when faced with a decision about money, the believer can look to the tenth commandment about coveting and ask, "Am I desiring this possession at the expense of others?" When making decisions about relationships, the sixth commandment reminds the believer of the value of human life and the importance of honoring others with their words and actions.

Living the Law in the Context of Grace

Finally, it is important to remember that the moral law is not a means of salvation but a guide for living out the believer's new identity in Christ. The New Covenant frees the believer from the condemnation of the law but does not abolish its relevance. The believer's obedience to the law is a response to God's grace, not an attempt to earn favor with Him.

As Ephesians 2:8–10 explains, "For it is by grace you have been saved, through faith—and this is not from yourselves, it is the gift of God—not by works, so that no one can boast. For we are God's handiwork, created in Christ Jesus to do good works, which God prepared in advance for us to do." Our good works, which include obeying the law, are the result of God's grace at work in us through the Holy Spirit, and they are a testimony to the world of His love and holiness.

Conclusion: The Law as a Guide to Spiritual Maturity

The law continues to be relevant for the believer's life today. It serves as a guide that points to God's character, helping the believer to live in accordance with His will. The Holy Spirit empowers the believer to live in obedience to God's commands, and this obedience reflects the love and gratitude that come from having our being transformed by God's grace.

The law is a gift to believers, not a burden, and it helps us grow in spiritual maturity to live in a way that reflects God's holiness and leads to flourishing in all areas of life.

Study Guide for Chapter 16

Practical Application for Today:
Understanding the Role of the Law in the Believer's Life

Summary:
The Law guides ethical living, shaped by grace and empowered by the Spirit.

Discussion Questions:

1. Why is obedience impossible apart from grace?

2. How does the Law reflect God's character?

3. Where do you sense the Spirit leading toward deeper obedience?

Application:

Choose one commandment to intentionally practice this week.

Scripture Reflection: Galatians 5:22–25

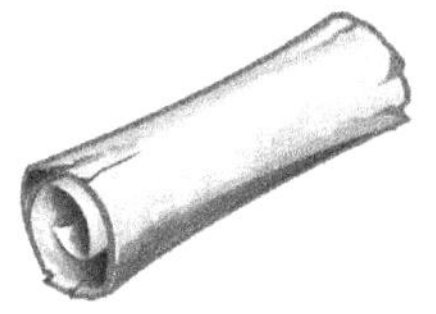

Epilogue:

A LEGACY OF OBEDIENCE: "BE CAREFUL TO OBEY"

Old Testament Passages

Deuteronomy 4:6 – "Observe them carefully, for this will show your wisdom and understanding to the nations."

Deuteronomy 6:3 – "Hear, Israel, and be careful to obey so that it may go well with you and that you may increase greatly in a land flowing with milk and honey, just as the Lord, the God of your ancestors, promised you."

Deuteronomy 8:1 – "Be careful to follow every command I am giving you today, so that you may live and increase and may enter and possess the land the Lord promised on oath to your ancestors."

Deuteronomy 11:22 – "If you carefully observe all these commands I am giving you to follow—to love the Lord your God, to walk in obedience to him and to hold fast to him."

Deuteronomy 12:28 – "Be careful to obey all these regulations I am giving you, so that it may always go well with you and your children after you, because you will be doing what is good and right in the eyes of the Lord your God."

Deuteronomy 17:19 – "It is to be with him, and he is to read it all the days of his life so that he may learn to revere the Lord his God and follow carefully all the words of this law and these decrees."

Joshua 1:7 – "Be strong and very courageous. Be careful to obey all the law my servant Moses gave you; do not turn from it to the right or to the left, that you may be successful wherever you go."

1 Kings 2:3 – "And observe what the Lord your God requires: Walk in obedience to him, and keep his decrees and commands, his laws and regulations, as written in the law of Moses."

1 Chronicles 28:8 – "So now I charge you in the sight of all Israel and of the assembly of the Lord, and in the hearing of our God: Be careful to follow all the commands of the Lord your God, that you may possess this good land and pass it on as an inheritance to your descendants forever."

Psalm 119:4 – "You have laid down precepts that are to be fully obeyed."

Jeremiah 29:4–7 (letter to the exiles) – "This is what the Lord Almighty, the God of Israel, says to all those I carried into exile from Jerusalem to Babylon: 'Build houses and settle down; plant gardens and eat what they produce . . . seek the peace and prosperity of the city to which I have carried you into exile.'"

Jeremiah 29:12 (God promises to bring the exiles back after seventy years, as a result of their obedience) – "Then you will call on me and come and pray to me, and I will listen to you."

Ezekiel 36:26–27 (promise of a new heart) – "I will give you a new heart and put a new spirit in you; I will remove from you your heart of stone and give you a heart of flesh. And I will . . . move you to follow my decrees and be careful to keep my laws."

Jeremiah 31:33 – "'This is the covenant I will make with the people of Israel after that time,' declares the Lord. I will put my law in their minds and write it on their hearts. I will be their God, and they will be my people."

New Testament Passages

Matthew 5:19 – Jesus teaches, "Therefore, anyone who sets aside one of the least of these commands and teaches others accordingly will be called least in the kingdom of heaven, but whoever practices and teaches these commands will be called great in the kingdom of heaven."

Matthew 7:21 – "Not everyone who says to me, 'Lord, Lord,' will enter the kingdom of heaven, but only the one who does the will of my Father who is in heaven."

Matthew 28:19–20 (the Great Commission) – Jesus commands His disciples to "go and make disciples of all nations . . . teaching them to obey everything I have commanded you."

John 14:15 – "If you love me, keep my commands."

John 14:23–24 – "Anyone who loves me will obey my teaching . . . Anyone who does not love me will not obey my teaching."

Romans 6:16 – "Don't you know that when you offer yourselves to someone as obedient slaves, you are slaves of the one you obey—whether you are slaves to sin, which leads to death, or to obedience, which leads to righteousness?"

Romans 12:1–2 – "Therefore, I urge you, brothers and sisters, in view of God's mercy, to offer your bodies as a living sacrifice, holy and pleasing to God—this is your true and proper worship. Do not conform to the pattern of this world, but be transformed by the renewing of your mind."

Philippians 2:12 – "Therefore, my dear friends, as you have always obeyed—not only in my presence, but now much more in my absence—continue to work out your salvation with fear and trembling."

Hebrews 5:9 – "And, once made perfect, he became the source of eternal salvation for all who obey him."

James 1:22 – "Do not merely listen to the word, and so deceive yourselves. Do what it says."

1 John 2:3, 6 – "We know that we have come to know him if we keep his commands. Whoever claims to live in him must live as Jesus did."

ACKNOWLEDGMENTS

As I sit here at Corners End, as we call our little oasis north of Atlanta, I am humbly aware of the many tools God has used to craft me. It started with Vernon and Rose Lutz who welcomed me into a special, totally functional family of origin, for which I am so thankful.

And thank you to the educators who invested in me at Calvert Hall High School; the University of Maryland, Baltimore County; and Covenant Theological Seminary. Professor John Sanderson of Covenant Theological Seminary instilled in me what has become the lifelong thrill of reading the Scriptures as God intended them to be read. He also began my initial fascination with a proper biblical understanding of the Decalogue.

Thank you to Randy Schlichting, President of Metro Atlanta Seminary, as well as to the many students there where I had the opportunity to test out many of the concepts and frameworks discussed in this book.

Thank you to each of the godly business leaders who allowed me to walk alongside them through the organization of Convene. The staff and chairs there who make it easy for me to do so. Each of them in their own unique way were instrumental in my developing real-life wisdom tools as they went about becoming wise.

And of course, special thanks to my wife of fifty years, who not only bore 63 total pounds of Lutz children but who was active in developing them into the seven wholesome individuals of whom we could not be prouder.

And finally, thank you to my sixteen beautiful grandchildren who permit me to test out these ideas on the next generation.

ABOUT THE AUTHOR

Thomas P. Lutz is President of Vision Planners, LLC, Chair of Convene in Atlanta, and Professor of Biblical Studies at Metro Atlanta Seminary. A graduate of the University of Maryland (Classical Languages) and Covenant Theological Seminary (M.Div., D.Min.), Tom founded a Reformed Presbyterian Church in Baltimore before launching a global construction-information firm that grew to $120 million in revenue across 18 countries. He later founded Vision Planners to help churches, nonprofits, and businesses realize their visions. Author of *Equipping Christians for Kingdom Purpose in Their Work*, Tom lives in Peachtree Corners, GA, with Sherry, his wife of 50 years, their 7 adult children and their 16 grandchildren

www.ingramcontent.com/pod-product-compliance
Lightning Source LLC
LaVergne TN
LVHW050648100826
845148LV00011B/2034

* 9 7 8 1 6 8 4 8 8 1 7 2 7 *